PRAISE FOR
Growth Strategies for the Hungry Entrepeneur

"A fascinating narrative with high energy of personal experiences and insights on how to re-source oneself with passion and perseverance as we are at the source of all we do. A heartfelt sharing by Trish Mandewo that exhorts constant learning and courageous exploration. This book gives the gentle comfort of companionship, understanding and wisdom en route the challenging journey of entrepreneurship."

Dr. Harbeen Arora – Founder, BIOAYURVEDA and Global Chairperson, ALL Ladies League (ALL) & Women Economic Forum (WEF)

"In Growth Strategies for the Hungry Entrepreneur, Trish Mandewo shares hints, tips, and strategies for success through the lens of her own journey as an entrepreneur. Her own personal stories, complemented by topic experts, provide insight and guidance that will help any small or medium size business avoid common pitfalls and thrive."

Dana Harvey – Founder, Dana Harvey Communications

"Trish is a passionate entrepreneur who has generously dedicated her time to helping and motivating others navigate the waters of business. Her legacy as a business mentor has positively impacted both seasoned and upcoming entrepreneurs. Her steadfast commitment to sharing her knowledge and uplifting others is reflected in this book. I have no doubt that many will be inspired and indeed benefit from this book."

Jessie Adcock – Digital Transformation and Global Technology Executive

"Passionate, personable, intelligent, driven, organized, excited to share her knowledge: these are enduring qualities of this author who I have personally known for more than a quarter-century. This book is a display and expression her experience and qualities as she lays out for the reader what she has learned in starting and running successful businesses. Any interested and motivated reader can also use the tips. It is straightforward, highly readable, interesting and useful. I highly recommended this book."

William David Austin – RN BSN

GROWTH STRATEGIES FOR THE HUNGRY ENTREPRENEUR

Trish Mandewo

Copyright © 2019 by Trish Mandewo

All rights reserved. No part of this book may be reproduced, stored in a retrieval system or transmitted, in any form or by any means, without the prior written consent of the publisher or a licence from The Canadian Copyright Licensing Agency (Access Copyright). For a copyright licence, visit www.accesscopyright.ca or call toll free to 1-800-893-5777.

ISBN 978-1-6930-78-0 (paperback)

Produced by Bright Wing Media

www.brightwing.ca

Cover design by Rose Kapp

DEDICATION

I dedicate this book to my loving husband Alexander Mandewo and my beautiful daughter Alexandra (Lexi) Mandewo for their unwavering love and support. You are my inner circle and my Ohana.

I would also like to dedicate this book to my family starting with my late father, Cyril Mupfuuri Masenda, who was my greatest teacher and mentor. My Mom, Matilda Masenda, my rock and my comfort. Thank you for showing me what leadership is all about Mom. To my late sisters Lorna, Josephine and Clare, this one is for you. You were my biggest cheerleaders and you encouraged me to go after my dreams. My sisters Stella, Anna and Kanu, thank you for being pillars in my life.

Lastly, to all entrepreneurs out there especially those from humble beginnings and those fighting to stay afloat and to all those who are thinking of becoming entrepreneurs: may this book give you some comfort! Yes, running a business can be a lonely and tedious journey, but you don't have to go at it alone.

CONTENTS

DEDICATION	5	
ACKNOWLEDGEMENTS	7	
PROLOGUE	9	
ONE	The P-cubed Method for Success	13
TWO	Characteristics of a Successful Entrepreneur	18
THREE	Communication Strategies for Entrepreneurs	24
FOUR	Networking for Success	31
FIVE	Obtaining Capital	44
SIX	Risk & Finance	56
SEVEN	Marketing Strategies for Success	62
EIGHT	Social Media Strategy for Success	71
NINE	Know Your Personal Brand	79
TEN	Mentoring for Success	85
ELEVEN	Human Capital	92
TWELVE	Taking Care of Your Biggest Asset	96
THIRTEEN	Emotional Intelligence for Business Success	102
FOURTEEN	Trish's Toolbox	114
EPILOGUE	126	
AUTHOR'S BIOGRAPHY	127	

ACKNOWLEDGEMENTS

To the team that came together to make this book a success, I thank you and I love you all.

Contributors

Catherine Steele – Owner & CEO of *English Pronunciation For Success*

Cecilia Mkondiwa – Executive In Residence at *Women's Enterprise Centre*; Vice President of Operations at *Tiderise Technologies Inc.*

Jill Earthy – Head of *Female Funders at Powered by Highline*

Rita Kim – CEO at *Partners for Growth Advisory Services Inc.*

Angela Bains – Strategic Director at *TransformExp*, Keynote Speaker & Educator at *BCIT*

Diana Bishop – Founder of *The Success Story Program*

Christina Anthony – Founder & Chair Emeritus of *Forum for Women Entrepreneurs (FWE)*

Jennifer McKinnon – Owner of *Creating Culture*

Kanu Jacobsen – CEO at *Candle Consulting*; Host of *Real Love Real Stories Podcast*

Sandra Horton – CEO & Owner at *Horton Collaborations*; Co-founder of *Women's Collaborative Hub Society*

Editors

Margaret Jetelina – Writer & Editor in *Metro Vancouver*

Hannah Mondiwa – Digital Storyteller; Writer and Intercultural Communications Specialist

PROLOGUE

I have always had a fascination for elephants. Researchers have proven that elephants are exceptionally smart. They have three times as many neurons as humans, are excellent communicators, very empathetic and can identify and mimic human voices. Best of all, they have excellent memory as this is critical to their survival in the wild. Entrepreneurs can learn a lot from these gentle giants. My hope is that the information in this book will help you transform your business so you can become a gentle giant in your own way.

You will notice that I also use a lot of tennis analogies. Why you might ask? In addition to loving elephants, I love tennis! I am an avid and devoted player and I believe that we can all learn a lot from the game. Looking at me you would never guess that I am a tennis player. I recall many times when I played in tournaments and my opponents walked onto the court thinking they had already won. What they didn't realize is that I have learned the art of winning; I might not appear physically tough, but I am mentally tough. I also have the finesse and game intelligence needed to win at my level. There are a lot of parallels between tennis and running a business as you will learn in my book.

The Hungry Entrepreneur has a strong desire or craving for success. This hunger for success is synonymous with hunger for knowledge and hunger to be a better person than one was the previous day. This book feeds the entrepreneur's appetite.

What to expect from this book.

This book will teach you the art of being a successful businessperson. It integrates my personal entrepreneurial journey as well as perspectives from other industry experts while discussing a variety of key business topics. I will also openly share the challenges and wins I have experienced in my own business journey.

This book is meant to empower both aspiring entrepreneurs and those who are already running their own businesses. The skills in the book will help you start your business strong or up the ante on your current enterprise.

In a nutshell, you will get the proven strategies to running a success business, complete with my "P-cubed" rules.

I am because we are: Ubuntu / Hunhu

I was born and raised in the township of Highfield in Harare, Zimbabwe. One of the precepts for the Shona people is *Hunhu*, also know as *Ubuntu* in other parts of Southern Africa. *Hunhu* is a magical word that encompasses all humanity, it emphasizes the importance of human kindness. I learned to live by this traditional African philosophy that offers an understanding of ourselves in relation to the world. According to *Ubuntu*, there exists a common bond between us all and it is through our interactions with our fellow human beings that we discover our own human qualities. The term finds a clear expression in the Zulu/Nguni/Ndebele phrase: *umuntu ngumuntu ngabantu*, meaning a person is a person through other persons; we affirm our humanity when we acknowledge that of others. My parents instilled *Ubuntu* in my sisters and me. To this day, I use *Ubuntu* in my day-to-day life and in business.

I remember the story of a foreign worker who visited a village in the Tonga area of Zimbabwe. As was often the case with foreigners, he brought candy from his home country. He decided to play a game with the kids: placing a basket of candy under a tree and making the kids line up about 100 metres away, he told the kids to race to the bowl. Whoever got to the bowl first was to enjoy all the candy by themselves. The kids lined up nicely, and the man yelled "GO." and the kids looked at each other, held hands, walked together to the bowl and divided the candy equally among themselves. When the gentleman asked them why they did so, they giggled and answered "*Ubuntu*". The kids knew that there was enough candy for all of them to enjoy so there was no need to compete. Entrepreneurship is not any different. Ubuntu can be translated to mean collaboration; any business becomes successful because of the people who believe in the product or service. A business cannot and will not survive in isolation.

Don't be a Statistic

When I started my Tumblebus business, a mobile kids' gym franchise, I had policy and procedure manuals complete with a marketing and sales plan from Tumblebus USA through Tumblebus Canada. None of the information was relevant nor effective in my area; Vancouver was a completely different market. Vancouver clients and their needs were totally different from those in Eastern Canada or the United States. I continued on the path, but because I had an open mind and I was flexible, I made many changes along the way. I experienced exponential growth and I avoided becoming a statistic of failed small businesses.

- A few important facts to keep in mind:
- 20 per cent of small businesses fail in their first year
- 30 per cent of small business fail in their second year
- 50 per cent of small businesses fail after five years in business
- 70 per cent of small business owners fail in their 10th year in business.[1]

---

1 Fundera.com

- Small to medium-sized enterprises (SMEs) account for 97.9 per cent of business in Canada[2], 97.6 per cent in the United States[3] and 99.9 per cent in the United Kingdom[4].

My Promise to You

I promise that you will learn how to avoid being a statistic and the tricks to help you run your business successfully. In fact, you will learn how to run your small business as a big business. Here is to your success!

---

2   Industry Canada www.ic.gc.ca/eic/site/061.nsf/eng/h_03090.html#point1-1

3   SBE Council https://sbecouncil.org/about-us/facts-and-data/

4   Business statistics by Chris Rhodes

The P-cubed Method for Success

For many people, starting a business is a scary and daunting task. The risk of losing always lingers as there are so many unknowns to deal with. Having feelings of fear is normal. My P-cubed method will help you overcome those fears.

One of my all-time favourite books is Simon Sinek's *Start with Why*. Simon's Start With Why movement is all about getting people to be inspired by the work they do. Knowing why we do what we do is very important, and a look at the world's most successful people reveals that they all started with their Why: the Wright brothers, Jeff Bezos and Steve Jobs are great examples. My Why is summarized by my P-cubed formula - Passion, Purpose and Plan.

P-cubed Rule #1 — Passion

The dictionary defines passion as an intense emotion, a compelling enthusiasm or desire for something. Many people question whether passion is good for business or not. In my opinion, passion is a must; launching a business just to make money or to simply fill a gap in the market like in my Tumblebus case will likely result in failure. Richard Branson said it best when he remarked, "Passion is one of the most effective motivators when it comes to launching a business and often one of the strongest predictors of whether an idea will lead to success. He calls this the "aha!" idea.

When I set my goal to leave Zimbabwe in search of a better life in 1989, I was not thinking of what my passion was. My goal was about breaking the cycle of poverty. My career choice was two-pronged: the first was which profession was going to make me rich as quickly as possible, and the second was to fulfill my grandmother's death wish for me to be a doctor. On her death bed, my grandmother's last words to me were: "You are smart. One day, you are going to be like these doctors who have been taking care of me." For these reasons, I set my sights on becoming a physician, and so I majored in pre-med biology at Oklahoma Baptist University (OBU).

I graduated from OBU in a record three years and passed the Optometry Admission Test (OAT) on the first go. I received acceptance letters from the University of New England College of Optometry and the University of Houston College of Optometry. My dream of being an ophthalmologist and running my own private clinic was quickly deferred due to lack of finances. As a foreign student, I was awarded academic scholarships, but they were insufficient, and I had no other financial sources. Grants and loans were not an option as a foreign student. Looking back, I see that perhaps this dream never actualized because it was never my passion. I was going into this profession for all the wrong reasons.

I've learned that it's much easier to harness your passion and turn it into profit. Moreover, building your business around your passion eliminates fear as there is a feeling that even if the business fails, at least you are doing something you love.

P-cubed Rule #2 — Purpose

Growing up, my father instilled in me the lesson that partaking in anything without a purpose is like going on an endless journey. It is critical to treat this journey as an expedition and to approach the voyage with an open and curious mind.

In this journey we call life, purpose is like a navigation map. You simply set your destination and then you add the cardinal points and map out how you want to get to your final destination. The magic comes when you can align your passion with your purpose. Let's be honest, many of us have gifts and talents but only a few of us nail down what our gifts are, let alone utilize them effectively.

This will sound weird to many, but growing up, my purpose was to "be the boy that my father never had." My father had seven girls and no sons in a culture that was very patriarchal. There was the belief that girls were useless as they could not carry the family name, would not help their parents in their old age as they would marry off and be controlled by their husbands. From a very young age, I set out to prove them wrong: I was going to get an education, be a businesswoman and, of course, take care of my parents in their old age.

I look back and feel sorry for young me as that was such a grandiose purpose and burden for a young girl to carry. In the end, I turned out okay and I was, and still am, able to take care of my mom. My dad passed away a proud dad as well.

Millennials are doing a much better job with aligning their businesses or careers with their purpose. Studies show that 50 per cent of millennials are willing to take a pay cut so they can follow a meaningful path aligned with their purpose. Many are starting their businesses this way. Many of my fellow GenXers and baby boomers are still searching for their purpose. Better late than never, eh? From a company's perspective, purpose is the driving force that enables it to define its true brand and create its unique culture.

A purpose statement is not a vision, mission or value statement; it should express your organization's impact on the lives of your customers and clients. It should also inspire your staff to do the work. In a nutshell, your company's purpose is its identity, a bold affirmation of its being in purpose.

P-cubed Rule #3 — Plan

We all know that failing to plan means planning to fail. When I write speeches about the importance of planning, I often start by sharing my tennis stories. Tennis is a very interesting game, when players walk on the court, they have a plan. Most of the time the plan is to stick to the game plan and not to play the opponent's game. In doubles, when the partners huddle, they always remind each other to stick to the plan. I remember a league match that my doubles partner Kuniko and I lost after winning the first set and leading 5-2 in the second set. We had a plan to be aggressive. The plan was working nicely, and we were winning easily so we relaxed and became lax. The other team had been lobbing from the get-go, but our aggressive game play was disruptive to them. When we relaxed, we started lobbing back and lobbing was not our strength. We started losing points, then games. They started gaining confidence and making shots they were not making before. They won the second set. By the third, we were getting nervous and our shots were slipping away; we started making more errors and we eventually lost the match. In hindsight, we realized the other team took us away from our game; we started playing their game and we abandoned our plan in the second set.

Without a plan, one can quickly lose. Many tennis players walk off the court wondering what happened; in fact, they secretly wish they could start the game over. Business is no different.

Remember the statistics of failed business I referred to earlier? Those business owners often look back and wish they had built a solid plan or that they had followed their plan.

Many people set out to become entrepreneurs without a plan in place. Simply wanting to make money is not a plan. When you plan a trip, you know where you are going, how you are getting there, and you have an idea of what you want to do while you are there. Business is no different the who, what, when, where, and why are critical parts of building a successful business.

When we let our inner voice lead us to the path with passion and purpose, we are free, and when we ignore that voice, we are prisoners in our own bodies.

Trish Mandewo

TWO

Characteristics of a Successful Entrepreneur

Quite often I get invited to speak to youth, new business owners and new immigrants on what it takes to be an entrepreneur. In all honesty, these groups are not the only ones who need to know what I have to share. I have friends who have dreamed of being entrepreneurs, but they keep avoiding the challenge as they feel they are not made for it.

I am sure you have also heard people say that entrepreneurship is not for everyone or that entrepreneurs are wired differently. There isn't any ideal personality, but there are certain qualities that most entrepreneurs do possess. You could have all, some or just one of the qualities, there is no magic formula.

I like to say I was born to be an entrepreneur. I am not sure if this is true or if it's a case of circumstances shaping my future. I was born into a family that had lots of love and not much at all on the financial side. When I was seven years old, I started a candle-selling business. I had received some money over the Christmas holidays, $2 to be exact. I decided to ask my dad if he could buy something for me to sell in the community and he suggested candles. I remember a pack of 10 cost 65 cents; if you bought more boxes, the price was 45 cents. In our community, electric power was not dependable, and there were blackouts many nights. Candles were, therefore, a necessary commodity. Dad bought four packs for me and that night there was a blackout. I asked my sister Clare to accompany me in the thick darkness of the night to sell the candles. We took off around the block shouting "Candles! 10 cents, 10 cent candles." I can still hear my high-pitched, soft and innocent voice as we went around the neighbourhood. We sold all our candles in less than two hours. This was the start of my candle-selling business.

I was making good money for a seven-year-old. My sisters and the adults on our street started borrowing my money to make ends meet before pay day. I told them I would lend them the money if they would pay me more in return. They were always so desperate, so they agreed to my terms. I, unbeknownst to me, became a loan shark. I remember demanding double sometimes. Once, my sister Anna and my cousin did not pay me as scheduled so I took one shoe from each of them, the only pair of school shoes they had, and hid them in the garden by the bushy sugar canes. I only gave them back the shoes after they'd paid me back. Don't ask me how and where I learned to be that way at such a tender age. If you are to learn anything from this story, learn the courage and the entrepreneurial spirit that this seven-year-old had. I am happy to say, that spirit is still very much alive in me.

Many studies have looked at the traits of entrepreneurs and many more are still in the pipeline. The biggest question is why fewer women get into business. Women, in general, possess may of the said traits and yet they are underrepresented in business. One of the driving forces for me writing this book is the hope that it will give courage to those women contemplating whether they should get into business or not, and that it will help those already in business to excel.

Below are the qualities that I normally share when I speak to the aforementioned groups:

- **Being true to yourself.** Many women feel that to be successful, they have to have the stereotypical aggressive male attitude. There is no need to conform yourself to this idea of what a leader should be like. Aim to be the confident leader that you are.

- **Own your successes.** I know many women are modest and constantly downplay their strengths. This is probably because other women can be very quick to judge and label other women in power. I challenge you to allow yourself to unleash your greatness.

- **Embrace failure.** Failure is the roadmap to success. Do not fear it, learn from every mistake you make.it.

- **Give yourself permission to be the difference you want to see in the world.** You are greater than you can imagine. Rather than waiting for someone else to be the champion, raise your hand and be that person. Do not allow limiting beliefs to hold you back. Be still and look within to rid yourself of those blocks. Allow yourself to move on and get what's yours. In other words, grab your wings.

- **Don't let your past define you.** This one is big for me. When I start drowning myself with the past, I go to my favourite quote by Nelson Mandela: "As I walked out the door toward the gate that would lead to my freedom, I knew if I didn't leave my bitterness and hatred behind, I'd still be in prison." When I find myself looking in the rear-view mirror, I do the following:

  » I use the 15 seconds rule. I give any thoughts that come to mind 15 seconds and I acknowledge them and move on to the endless possibilities that lie ahead. I realize that although I cannot change my past, I can, however, control my thoughts and how I choose to deal with the history.

» I make it a point to be conscious of my present thoughts and feelings.

» I stay conscious of any self-sabotaging thoughts. When my business was picking up and big contracts were flowing in, the "poor little girl" voices would surface. Having money was for others, not for me. I couldn't fathom having that much money, what would I do with it? And so, I would self-sabotage. Instead of signing the contract and sending it in, I would come up with a million reasons not to. I remember calling clients and offering them further discounts because I felt guilty about making that much money.

» I am an opportunity crusader. When others see problems, I see opportunities.

Here is a short list of qualities and traits that many successful entrepreneurs share. Put a check mark on the ones that you possess. Perhaps you can take note of the ones you would like to work on.

- ❏ Hardworking
- ❏ Open-minded
- ❏ Charismatic
- ❏ Hungry
- ❏ Decisive
- ❏ Self disciplined
- ❏ Persistent
- ❏ Ambitious
- ❏ Passionate
- ❏ Determine

- ❏ Creative
- ❏ Competitive
- ❏ Confident
- ❏ Disciplined
- ❏ Empathetic
- ❏ Good listener
- ❏ Visionary
- ❏ Daring
- ❏ Action-oriented
- ❏ Process-oriented

Once you have gained the courage, I recommend that you then apply my P-cubed method as discussed earlier, rid yourself of any fears and concerns, and go after your entrepreneurial dreams.

> The only way to achieve your entrepreneurial goals is to get rid of the fear of failure and take the leap.
>
> **Trish Mandewo**

Communication Strategies for Successful Entrepreneurs

I was born in Zimbabwe, but my parents' origins are in South Africa and Malawi. My daughter was born in the United States, but we are now Canadians. Our history is simple compared to some I have encountered. The Sanskrit phrase "*Vasudhaiva Kutumbakam*" means "the world is one family." This phrase is slowly becoming true as people from all over the world migrate to other countries. The diversity in today's world makes it complex, but the English language is often the glue as English has fast become the most widely used language in the entire world, especially in business and trade. English is vital for success and is the most sought-after language in the corporate world.

Many second language learners find English tough to learn, in fact, even native speakers find English hard. The English language vocabulary has Germanic, French and Latin origins. For non-native speakers, homonyms (words that sound the same, but have different meanings), generational terms, idioms, pronunciation, grammar and spelling all make it complicated. While at university, I came out of my bedroom after a night of sleep on my new sheets and announced that "my sheets were so smooth." My housemates Rita, Traci and Beth looked at each other and burst laughing. I did not understand what was so funny. They repeated the phrase and laughed even more.

25

I was getting upset, and eventually they shared that the word "sheets" was coming out as "shits." To date, I struggle with this word. Can you imagine walking into a board room and not being understood?

Communication is a vital life skill no matter what you are doing. As a double's tennis player, I value a partner who communicates. In tennis, communication is the key to winning a match. My husband and I play a lot of mixed doubles tournaments. In fact, for years, we used to drive to Kansas City for a couple's doubles tournament. Our strategy was always to split the couples by putting the ball in the middle. The couples who communicated, did well. Without fail, the non-communicators always fought. You would hear phrases like: "That was mine, NO! that was mine! Why didn't you get that? It was on your forehand! But you didn't say yours! You didn't say mine! ..." You get what I mean. In a doubles match, lack of communication quickly turns into a blaming game.

There is no doubt that clear and effective communication is important for all aspects of business. My communications training started in the church at an early age, I loved the pulpit; I would volunteer to teach or preach at any opportunity I got. As an adult, I turned to Toastmasters. Toastmasters has taught me how to become a more effective communicator, how to improve my grammar and vocabulary, be a great listener and manage my time.

Elephants communicate using infrasonic sounds, mothers and babies use trunks to communicate through touch. When frustrated by lack of social interaction, they move slowly and bob their heads. We can learn a lot from these gentle giants. Entrepreneurs not only need to be good communicators, they also need to be effective communicators, as that is how they share and present ideas clearly with staff, team members, clients and colleagues.

I turned to my good friend Catherine Steele who is a pronunciation expert and works with many entrepreneurs and business leaders. I asked Catherine to share tips on how all of us global citizens can improve our communication.

COMMUNICATION FOR ENTREPRENEURS

By Catherine Steele

Communicating well as an entrepreneur means paying attention to details that the average person never needs to think about.

Which of the following best describe your speaking style? Do you have:

- Such clear speech that you never need to repeat yourself.
- Enhanced listening skills that are superior to your competition.
- Cultural awareness that goes beyond your first culture.
- Knowledge of when to use more elegant and more casual language styles.
- A large enough vocabulary to adapt to any circumstance.
- Confidence sharing humorous anecdotes.
- Strategies to handle communication breakdowns.
- Resources to boost your speaking confidence.

Throughout my career as a speaker, pronunciation coach and global talent support strategist, I have identified a number of unique communication challenges facing entrepreneurs.

1. **Clear speech** can mean the difference between a thriving business and bankruptcy. It's essential to be crystal clear to:

- sell your products and services
- ask for funding

- network
- represent your business as an event sponsor

Who hasn't been to a networking event where "Carl" missed out on his 30 seconds of fame because not everyone in the room could understand him?

Tip: Use pacing to your advantage. It gives your listener time to adjust to the sound of your English and to ask questions for clarification.

2. Representing your own business requires specialized **listening skills** to adjust to the variety of questions, opinions and styles of English in:

- sales calls
- meetings with your team
- discussions with suppliers
- expert panel discussions

It is essential to become familiar with the way your clients and suppliers express themselves in English to be able to conduct business over the phone.

Have you ever been in a situation where input was requested and "Ana," the expert in the field, failed to catch what was being said and missed a golden opportunity to promote her business?

Tip: YouTube clips of top entrepreneurs in your community are great places to train your ear.

3. When you do business in a globally diverse community, **unwritten rules and cultural differences** can have unexpected negative effects on communication.

How often are you unsure of how to proceed when the culture is different from your own?

Tip: Watch movies from a variety of cultures and ask your global talent to offer insights.

4. As an entrepreneur, you are judged on the quality of your language skills. **Inappropriate levels of formality and negative intonation patterns** can lead to loss of credibility and clientele. The most successful entrepreneurs learn to be equally at ease at gala events and backyard barbecues.

How many events of each kind do you have on your calendar?

Tip: Go out and experience a variety of events. Follow the lead of people you respect.

5. With huge numbers of immigrants arriving each year, it is imperative that you be understood by people from all language backgrounds. **An extensive vocabulary** is required in order to accommodate the needs of different listeners. The ability to communicate quickly and easily with everyone you meet helps you build a solid business that doesn't rely on a single stream of traffic.

How many ways can you explain the key concepts in your business?

Tip: Use single Latin words to be brief and in writing and longer English phrases in conversation.

6. Connections you make through **networking with other businesses** will be the lifeblood of your business. When a respected member of the business community endorses your product or service, they are endorsing you. For this to happen, a personal relationship must be built on deeper conversations, successful interactions and humour.

Do you have five funny stories that you can call upon the way "Alex" does?

Tip: Humour requires attention to word stress, intonation and timing. Apply these skills to become an engaging person to speak to.

7. It's easy to understand how **miscommunication** can lead to poor

results, dangerous misunderstandings or conflict with your team. For entrepreneurs, miscommunication leads to:

- missed opportunities
- costly errors
- unhappy, unsupportive staff

Numbers are always a problem. In fact, you had trouble catching the last two numbers of "Lou's" phone number. Which parts of your own number are hard to understand?

Tip: Lengthen consonants and vowels to ensure that your numbers are crisp and clear.

8. The **personal toll** communication problems take on an entrepreneur include:

- loss of self-confidence
- personal and professional embarrassment
- the burden of re-establishing a damaged brand

What strategies do you have in place to handle communication problems?

Tip: Surround yourself with excellent resources.

Once you know what to work on, systematically eliminate areas that damage your self-confidence. Build your speaking and listening strength through:

- podcasts
- conversation circles
- business mastermind groups
- public presentations
- Toastmasters

Personalized training solutions help you pinpoint those areas of weakness and are the best choice if you want to:

- benefit from flexible scheduling
- target your personal areas of concern
- systematically undo fossilized errors
- have your questions answered immediately?
- focus on vocabulary and phrasing that is specific to your industry

As you work on your business, schedule time to work on your own professional development. Clear speech, strong listening skills, cultural awareness, appropriate language formality, a powerful vocabulary, the ability to share anecdotes, strategies for handling communication breakdowns, and the support of resources that boost your speaking confidence will make you and your business unstoppable.

To your success!

"If elephants and ostriches can master the art of communication in the jungle, so can you."

Trish Mandewo

Networking for Success

The dictionary defines networking as the action or process of interacting with others to exchange information and develop professional or social contacts. In a nutshell, networking is all about building meaningful connections, sharing resources and creating opportunities.

When done well, networking helps you position your business for success. In fact, having a great network is gold as it is vital to business growth. I view networking as currency. I often remind people that they should not confuse networking with selling. Effective networking requires sweat equity and patience as there is no magic wand or a quick way to go about it.

With all my businesses, I have never had the luxury of a sales and marketing budget. I was the sales and marketing specialist and the only currency I had was my time. This led me to become a networking specialist. All my business successes are directly related to the amount of effective networking I did.

I started Vancouver Tumblebus three years after moving to Canada. I had no business or personal relationships to tap into. I had to build relationships from scratch. My strength is and always has been relationship building so I set out to network from Day One, and I attribute all my success to my networking skills.

For Tumblebus, I needed sponsors, so I networked with the big players and ended up with sponsorships from the likes of RBC, BMO, IG Financial and many more. Daycares were my clients, so I set out to network with child-minding professionals and owners.

Parents of kids 10 and under were also my clients so I made sure to find where the moms hung out and which events they attended. I joined moms' groups, attended children's expos, school events and everything in between.

By the third year in my business, my network was so huge that I was able to leverage the relationships and give a boost to my business. I sold my first license after four-and-a-half years.

Richard Branson said it best: "Business is all about personal contact. No matter how heavy your workload is ... everyone can and should be a networker."

Not to toot my own horn but I consider myself a networking specialist. I have been asked to speak on the topic numerous times and I have delivered many workshops and networking for success cafés. It is my pleasure to share my tried and true experiences.

Networking Opportunities

There are many different types of opportunities to network. Here are my top eight.

1. Professional associations such as those for accountants, lawyers, insurance professionals
2. Member based organized networking groups such as Board of Trades, Chambers of Commerce and Business Networking International (BNI)
3. Café-style facilitated networking with overarching topics of discussion
4. Community groups such as moms' groups and church groups

5. Online and social media networks

6. Speed networking: highly structured type of networking events in which participants move from table to table introducing their business and sharing business cards. The concept is modelled from speed-dating formats. It is often incorporated by other existing networking groups.

7. Master mind groups

8. Conventions and festivals. Networking opportunity are in the evenings or after the event ends.

Business networking is an effective low-cost marketing method for developing contacts, referrals and sales opportunities. As I mentioned earlier, I owe my business success to networking. It is, however, an art. Here are proven strategies on how to network for success:

- Have a specific plan for the networking event you are attending. Map out your agenda based on the people attending. Are you there to promote an upcoming event or your business in general? Are you looking for referrals or a mentor etc.? Be strategic in planning where and how you spend your time.

- Do your homework. If there is someone you absolutely want to connect with, show up early and sit at their table. If that's not possible, then ask someone else to introduce you.

- Choose the right networking group. Although you can always make meaningful business connections anywhere, know the purpose for all groups. Chambers of Commerce are for business connections, Rotary is for giving back to the community and book clubs are for your personal fulfillment.

- Be laser-focused and leave your ulterior motives at the door. First impressions are the last impressions when it comes to networking. Be present, in other words, be dedicated to the person in front of you. Do not look beyond the person nor move your eyes around the room! It's not about what's in it for you, but rather how you can help the other person.

- Everyone is important but NOT everyone is a great contact for you. Be cautiously selective.

- Offer to help and make sure you follow through. Remember, networking is about paying it forward. Choose to be a connector NOT a collector. You might not be able to help someone, but you know someone else who can. LinkedIn is a great tool to introduce people who have synergy.

- Be authentic and try by all means to avoid exaggerations.

- Always have a solid icebreaker. Don't depend on the other person for the conversation to flow. Ask open-ended questions such as who, what, where, why, when and how.

- Be mindful of the other person's time. Do not hog them. My rule of thumb is no more than three to five minutes per person. This allows you to introduce yourself and learn about the other person enough to determine if you should set up a follow-up meeting.

- Have a good closing. For example, "It was really a pleasure speaking to you. I am looking forward to learning more about your business." If they are a good fit, let them know you will contact them to set up a coffee or zoom call.

- Be selective with who you share your business cards with. Likewise, do not collect everyone's business cards. I like to take just a handful of business cards and keep them in my purse. I only pass them out to the select few. Also, avoid being a business card pusher, you know, the ones who are not interested in knowing you, all they want is to hand you their card and collect yours so they can spam you by selling you a sales pitch the next day. If you attend a meeting with a lot of pushers, graciously accept their card, but make sure to fold a corner on the cards you really want to follow up on. It makes it easier to sort when you get back to your office.

- Avoid being an onlooker. This is when two or three people are in a conversation and when you attempt to join them, they continue to have a conversation without drawing you in or acknowledging you. My rule of thumb is that you should hover over a conversation for 15 seconds to 30 seconds and then move on.
- Work hard on maintaining the relationships that you have built before you go out looking for more. Just think of all those key contacts you met and meant to follow up with, but you haven't gotten a chance.
- Have a post networking process. Mine is simple: I go to LinkedIn and look the person up, I then go to the person's personal as well as business Facebook (depending on the individual). After that I send them an email in which I briefly thank them for the conversation we had, and I specify where it was that we met. I then ask to set up an in-person meeting or a call.
- Calculate your Return on Investment (ROI) for any dollar or time you spend networking.

$$ROI = \frac{\text{Gain from Investment}}{\text{Cost of Investment}}$$

Networking Mistakes

Now that I have shared where and how to network, it is equally important to know the networking mistakes you should avoid.

- Be mindful not to set high expectations. The fact that you just met someone doesn't mean they are going to give you business.

- Avoid becoming a serial networker. This happens when you turn networking events into social events. You end up spending more time attending networking groups with no return on investment.

- Do not turn into a business card hoarder. If you fall into this trap, you will end up with boxes, bags or piles of business cards and have no idea what to do with them or where to start?

- Do not talk about yourself too much; this can turn people off you.

- Do not promise someone you are going to follow up with them and then don't. You will lose their trust.

- Please, please do not sell your product or service to the people you are networking with. You are there to build relationships.

- Avoid sounding desperate.

- Not having a social media presence. Social media can be overwhelming but it is important to choose one to be active on so others can find you if they forgot your business name.

- Make sure you have your business link on your social media, not doing so is like throwing a fishing rod with bait in the water and walking away.

- This one is critical: we all send emails to clients and potential clients; make sure you have a signature at the bottom of your email with your website link and phone number. If you have a social media presence, add links to as well.

- Don't be cocky. You might think your business is great and better than anyone else's in the room but remember there is always room for improvement. If the big wigs like Apple, Coca Cola and Microsoft think so, so should you.

- Avoid talking negatively about others; putting others or their business down says a lot about you.

- Don't forget the magic phrase: Thank you!

I would like to share the most common questions that attendees of my workshops ask. I hope they will address some of the questions you might also have.

Question: Where is the best place and time to network?

Answer: As a networker, you should be ready to build relationships at any given moment. In a checkout line, on the plane, at your child's birthday party, etc. If you are looking for organized networking, then the Top 10 list I shared earlier will be of great help.

Question: What quality do you think is the best for networking?

Answer: In my opinion, listening is the best quality that many appreciate. People are put off by those who are all about themselves. When networking, aim to listen twice as much as you talk.

Question: What is your recommendation for prep work before a meeting?

Answer Nothing irritates me more than people who make an appointment to meet someone and show up without any knowledge of the other person. To me, it's reflective that they are self-serving and are not interested in the other party at all. Check the other person's website and social media ahead of time, look up their company. Please do not show up with your 20 slides presentation.

Question: How can I show others that I am invested in them?

Answer: Successful networkers are always ready to help others. Share your experience and your contacts. Offer to make introductions.

Question: How important is networking on social media?

Answer: Based on the type of business you have; social media is critical. Check out more details in my social media strategy chapter.

Question: How important is body language when networking?

Answer: Your body language speaks volumes about you. Where you stand, how you stand, your hand gestures and eye contact all play a big role on how you are perceived. Your goal should be to come out as a confident, powerful, present, fun and welcoming individual.

Question: How do I start a conversation? I am introverted and find it hard?

Answer: Here are some icebreaker examples:

The simplest one is the classic weather small chat. Aren't we lucky to have this beautiful weather? How are you finding the temperature in this room?

- » Hi, my name is ...
- » Hi, I am interested in learning more about you and your organization.

- How did you hear about this event?

- You seem to know a lot of people here; do you network with this group often?

- Since we are both standing at the back, I feel I should introduce myself. My name is……

- Humour always works if its in you. Talk about something funny that you observed at the event or on your way.

- If joining two or more people: Mind if I join in? or How do you two know each other? These networking events can be so crazy. Mind if I join you over here where it's a little quieter?

Question: Is it okay to sell yourself when someone asks?

Answer: When someone asks you to share about yourself or your business, don't be bashful, start with your 30-second elevator pitch. Position yourself or your company as the expert that you are. This is your chance to shine. Remember to keep it short, sweet and to the point. This is not the time to tell the 10-minute story. Reputation and integrity are vital in developing trust. What do you want them to remember about you when they walk away?

Question: When is the best time to follow up?

Answer: Reliability and dependability are highly valued qualities in relationships. If you told someone you will be in touch or that you will connect them with someone, my rule of thumb is to do so within 24 hours. Doing so after weeks or months when someone has forgotten who you are is unacceptable and speaks to your character.

Question: What should I write when following up by email?

Answer: The subject line in your email is equally important as the content of the email. For the body, here are some tips:

- » Introduce yourself.
- » Remind the recipient of where you met them.
- » Make the next sentence about them.
- » Explain why you're reaching out.
- » Provide value for them.
- » State the call-to-action.
- » Thank them and sign off.

By now you probably know how much I love tennis metaphors. I happen to think that networking is like tennis, surprise! To be a good player, you must practice, practice, practice! When you finally get to play a match or tournament, you have to be patient with every point. Play creative and purposeful points, which will set you up for the win. Networking is no different; you must plant the seeds and then cultivate relationships over time; it calls for patience. At the end, the meaningful relationship brings in lots of value.

Remember that when it comes to networking, its quality over quantity. Aim to build real relationships because networking is really relationship building.

I will leave you with my "P" rules of networking summary:

- Be **P**resent in each conversation.
- Stay **P**ositive.
- **P**raise others.
- Activate your **P**lan.
- Be **P**atient.

Happy networking.

"Networking is a currency; invest in it wisely and the returns will be bountiful!"

Trish Mandewo

FIVE

Obtaining Capital

You have a brilliant business idea! Now, how do you get money to get it started? Or perhaps you already started your Small to Medium Enterprise (SME), but now you want to scale up. How and where do you access funding? Capital is the number one factor that stops many emerging entrepreneurs from bringing their business dreams to fruition.

The process of obtaining capital can be arduous to say the least. I have been fortunate to have successfully built a few businesses. My very first business was a home health agency in the United States. However, I used our family savings and almost bankrupted us in the process.

Depending on the type of business you have, the sales cycle might be long. In my home health case, the setup and sales cycles took almost two years. Certification and inspections took the bulk of the time, but, in the meantime, office doors had to be opened every day as per health inspection requirements. Not to mention that we could not see patients until the certification was done. I quit my day job so I could sit and wait as it didn't make sense to pay someone to do so. You can imagine the toll on finances.

My second business was a janitorial business, which I grew to 30 full-time employees and many part timers and contractors in eight years. As with the home health business, I did not borrow any capital. Had I known how or where to access capital; my business would have grown bigger in a shorter amount of time. The first two years were the toughest. I signed Oklahoma State University as client. I had to pay employees bi-weekly, but it would take three to five months for the university to pay me. Cash flow was a nightmare. The stress from this added pounds and grey hairs.

Looking back, I remember how lonely I was. I had no business network or support system. I made many assumptions based on my limited knowledge and stuck with them. One big assumption was that it was difficult to get capital, that banks would not approve small business loans. In my mind, this was true, so I didn't even try to seek capital. I had no mentor nor business advisor and I was navigating the road blindly and alone.

When we immigrated to Vancouver, I had had enough of entrepreneurship. I decided to go back to work in my field of embryology. Job searches indicated that jobs were abundant, so I was going to get hired in no time, right? Was I ever wrong! Finding a job in my field without "Canadian experience" would prove to be next to impossible. Evaluation of my credentials revealed that I needed to go back to the books because B.C. required Histology as part of the certification. Going back to school was not an option. I wanted to take care of our daughter.

I had to be creative. I remember sitting at the dining room table one day brainstorming with my husband about what we were going to do. Going to work in a general type of job was not an option either. We were listing possible business ideas and my daughter Alexandra (Lexi) who was six at the time said, "Well, no one is asking me what I think."

I turned to her and asked, "What do you think, baby girl?" We didn't realize that she had been listening intently and was very eager to share her thoughts. She responded, "You should have a Tumblebus." Her preschool, Pathways in Edmond, Oklahoma had the Tumblebus coming every other week and Lexi absolutely loved being on the Tumblebus. I told her that was a great idea, as I had not seen a single Tumblebus since moving to B.C. I quickly googled and there were no Tumblebuses at all in Canada. Someone had purchased one in Ontario five years prior, but it was not operating. My six-year-old was onto something. Exactly a year and half after that day, my daughter and I were going door to door to daycares doing market research as I had decided to bring the first-ever Tumblebus to Vancouver.

After establishing that Tumblebus would be a viable business, I knew I didn't want to wipe out our savings again, so I decided to pursue borrowing some of the capital for starting the business. I registered for a three-month course with Embers Venture. Embers brought in different speakers including one from a local bank who spoke about their small business loan and about their new immigrant loans. I was excited about the possibility of accessing capital.

Once I had completed my business plan, I applied for a business loan from Scotiabank since they were my main bank. After all, my first account in Canada was with Scotiabank. I quickly got a NO! The business loan manager said I had a brilliant and exciting business idea, but he was sorry, my loan wasn't approved. He proceeded to say, if I wanted to buy a boat or a plane, I would have had better chances because Scotiabank can always get the boat or plane back if I defaulted. I responded that I was going to have a Tumblebus that they could take. It won't be worth anything, he said. I truly wasn't going to win this argument.

I decided to approach Vancity. I applied for the small business loan at a local branch and the answer was NO! The reason this time was that I didn't own a home, so I had no collateral. The second reason was that Tumblebus was an unknown entity, so they had no figures to go by. I was left perplexed. If I was a McDonald's, it would be easy as they had a track record to go buy. As someone who doesn't give up easily, I continued to push my case stating that there were more than 300 Tumblebuses in the United States, all they had to do was call a few of them and get their proformas. The response was clear, they needed numbers from B.C. Once again, my hopes had been thwarted and I was devastated. Why were they not seeing the potential in this business?

Maybe the third time was to be the charm. I applied for a loan with RBC, and, again, the answer was NO. Just as I was giving up, the manager at RBC asked me if I had looked into women business loans from the government. This was music to my ears. I had no idea there was such a thing as women business loans. I asked for more information and he gave me details for Women's Enterprise Centre. I couldn't wait to contact them. That referral turned out to be the best thing that I got from the process. Two months later, I got a business loan from Women's Enterprise Centre and on February 9, 2013, Vancouver Tumblebus opened its doors for the first time.

Perhaps you already started your business and you are looking for a way to grow your business, or you want to start a business, how do you get funding? No matter where you are, visit the small business office in your community and ask them how you can access different streams of funding for business start-ups or for scaling your business.

Cecilia Mkondiwa of Women's Enterprise Centre was the account manager who came to my house to interview me for the loan. She has since become a very close friend and soul sister. I was happy to reach out to Cecilia for an insight into how women can get capital.

HOW TO GET START-UP CAPITAL FOR YOUR BUSINESS

By Cecilia Mkondiwa

Women are starting businesses at a faster rate than men, disrupting the norm and developing innovative platforms while facing institutional barriers. Financing the business is the biggest obstacle faced by women who are starting their own businesses. It is important to note that there are many different sources of financing: families, friends, banks, development lenders, angel investors, crowdfunding and more. Before you apply for financing, it is helpful to investigate your options to make sure your lender is the right fit for you and your business.

Financing Challenges for Women Business Owners

Women have many challenges in getting capital for their business. They:

- Are less comfortable with debt financing and less willing to take risks.
- Feel that traditional lenders often don't understand their distinct business goals, wants and needs. They do not fit in the mould sometimes.
- Lack visible role models and mentors to give them the confidence that they can do it.
- Need help figuring out how much money to ask for. On average, women apply for $60K in financing, compared to the $350K that men apply for.
- On average, grow more slowly and earn less than male-owned firms, which has ripple effects on their ability to succeed in obtaining financing.
- Are declined more often, due to the nature of the business (many women start service-based businesses, which have no assets to secure the loans), poor security and credit histories.

The good news: there is support specifically for women entrepreneurs.

Women's Enterprise Centre (WEC) is the leading business resource for existing and aspiring women business owners in B.C. Funded by the federal government since 1995, WEC has helped women with business loans, business skills training, personalized business advice, mentoring, practical resources and a supportive community.

Development Lenders:
Women's Enterprise Centre Business Loans

Women's Enterprise Centre is a development lender, which means they provide loans based on your business or growth plan. We are not a formula lender and we really try to look at all aspects of the business. As a government-funded not-for-profit, our goal is to help you be successful. We understand the unique needs of immigrants, so we personalize our service to suit your needs.

We also offer support to our loan clients. They are connected with a business advisor who offers personalized support, they can access our training programs for free and they can get matched with a mentor. This support is proven to improve our clients' chance of success. Over 75 per cent of our loan clients are still in business after five years, which is 50 per cent above the national average.

What You Need to Succeed in Securing Financing

To make sure you can access the financing you need from any lender, you will need several things:

1. **A viable business plan.** That means we should be able to read your business plan and thoroughly understand that it will be able to sustain itself, that it is profitable and will be able to compete successfully in the market. The trick with a business plan is to approach it one step at a time. Then it's more doable! WEC has many resources available to help you with this.

2. **A cash flow projection.** This will make you think, month-by-month, what money will be coming into and going out of your business. That includes *how* you will receive your sales revenues: cash at point of sale and/or accounts receivables over a 30- or 60-day period.

3. **Your resumé.** This shows a lender your skills, knowledge and experience as it relates to the business. If there are gaps, we

want to know how you will be addressing these.

4. **Equity.** Lenders want to see that you're investing in your own company. This could be cash that you're investing in your business now, equipment you already purchased, supplies that you've bought for the business. For existing businesses, this can be the equity on your balance sheet.

5. **Security/collateral.** Security is something you pledge to the lender so that if something unfortunate happens to the business and you can't pay the loan back, then the lender can resell it. Some examples of collateral are your car, house or equipment.

6. **A good credit rating.** Your credit history tells us about your character as it relates to your credit payment history. At WEC, we don't expect you to have a 5-star credit rating, but we need to consider how much debt you currently have. If you haven't done it before, it is good to check what is on your credit report. There are two main reporting organizations in Canada: Equifax Canada and Trans Union.

To learn more about WEC business loans program and view our current loan limit, interest rate, terms and conditions, visit wec.ca/businessloans.

Financing Options in Other Provinces: Women's Enterprise Initiative

WEC is part of the Women's Enterprise Initiative, which includes women's enterprise organizations in each of the Western provinces:

- Alberta Women Entrepreneurs (awebusiness.com)
- Women Entrepreneurs of Saskatchewan (wesk.ca)
- Women's Enterprise Centre of Manitoba (wecm.ca)

We are also part of the Women's Enterprise Organizations of Canada, which serve women business owners coast to coast. To find resources in your area, visit **weoc.ca**.

While getting a loan like I did is one option, there are many other options available. I reached out to another friend Jill Earthy, an accomplished entrepreneur who has successfully built and sold two companies. Jill uses her entrepreneurial drive to bring more women investors into the venture capital world. Here is what she shared in regard to alternative capital raising choices.

CAPITAL OPTIONS

By Jill Earthy

Capital is critical for business success. There are many ways to build your funding puzzle and to put the right pieces together for your unique funding needs.

It is important to explore the differences between debt and equity offerings, and traditional and new means of financing. Funding is not one size fits all, nor is it one way only, as many options fit together nicely.

Your decision will be based on your business model, stage of growth and the amount of funding you need. Some businesses are not eligible for debt financing as they are too early stage (without established traction) or do not have any assets to put against a loan as collateral. Some businesses may be eligible for a small portion of debt financing and may need to raise additional funding through investors to achieve the full amount of funding needed. Other companies are in fast-growth mode and want to bring on strategic investors, perhaps combined with some smaller investors.

First, understand why you are raising money. How do you plan to spend the funds over the next 12 months, and how will this money move your business forward? Outline a budget and identify key milestones you want to achieve.

Second, do your research. Talk to many different people and resources to understand how each program, including traditional loans, works, as well as the potential impact of bringing on external investors.

A new model to consider is online investment crowdfunding. This method is more inclusive by using technology to increase efficiencies and accessibility. For business owners, it offers an effective way to raise funds and to promote your business. Regulated platforms, such as FrontFundr, conduct a thorough review of the business and its viability, and work with the entrepreneurs collaboratively to set you up for success. If approved, the platform will work with you to develop your marketing strategy to increase your chances of success. Your business will then be publicly listed on the platform, enabling you to engage your network of customers, supporters and champions to invest in your business. This model is for Canada and it opens up access for any Canadian to participate, not just high net worth individuals as in the past. Around the world, there are similar models. The result can be funding as well as increased marketing exposure. It does take work and significant preparation but can be well worth it.

Individuals who are interested in investing can access information to make an informed decision and are then reviewed to ensure they understand the risks before processing the investment directly online. As a result, a new group of investors is emerging; a group that has been traditionally under-represented in investor circles. More Canadians want to invest in companies they believe in, and online investment crowdfunding can facilitate this.

There are many financing options available for businesses of all stages in Canada, and there are now new more efficient methods to access the right mix of financing for your business, including through online platforms. Understand your reasons for fundraising, and then be sure to consider all your options. You are the key to your business success, and you want to ensure you are bringing the right people and resources along with you.

While Cecilia and Jill's references are for Canada, there are similar organizations around the world. Simply go to the small business offices in your area or do google searches. You will find great information tailored to your area. You will also get access to workshops. Banks are aware of all the options available, but they often won't volunteer the information unless you probe, so ASK ASK ASK! Here are some suggestions on where to start in Canada, U.S., U.K. and South Africa.

Canada - www.ic.gc.ca/app/scr/innovation?lang=eng
U.S.A. - www.sba.gov/about-sba
U.K. - www.gov.uk/apply-start-up-loan
South Africa - www.entrepreneurmag.co.za/advice/funding/government-funding-funding/government-loans/

As an opportunity crusader, I specialize in asking questions.

Trish Mandewo

In tennis, the best players know when to take risks and when to play the safe shot. In business, risk management is what separates the best from the rest

Trish Mandewo

Risk & Finance

I like to say that risk and finance go together like a horse and carriage. For those of you who were fans of the ever so popular "Married with Children" TV show theme song from the 80s, you know about the horse-and-carriage reference. While it is great that there are many ways to access capital, there is a lot of risk associated.

Women are often risk averse, so we naturally stay away from borrowing. My first business Oasis Home Health and my second, Tru-Clean would have grown to being huge enterprises had I been open to borrowing. I had my own assumption of the huge risks and chose to stay away from borrowing. I can honestly share that this was my pitfall. Looking back, I wish I had more knowledge on how to take calculated risks. My good friend Rita Kim was happy to share some straight talk on risk and finance. Here is what she had to say.

A SIMPLE DEFINITION OF FINANCE
By Rita Kim

After working with over 10,000 companies from start-ups to international firms across industries, our team has created our own definition of finance. Regardless of whatever type of finance you are seeking, whether through your personal funds, investors or financial institutions, it all comes down to this simple definition:

FINANCE BOILS DOWN TO THE ABILITY OF BEING REPAID.

In order to get financing, there must be a clear understanding of your business, your end goals, your risks (and how they are mitigated), and how the loan or investment will be repaid. This is typically shown by a strong business plan with projections.

Let's put it another way to make it a bit easier to understand:

"Hey Trish, I've got this business idea and I'm telling you; this is the next big thing! Seriously! I just need $100,000 to move this forward and I promise that you will get paid back. Can you feel it? Are you with me? Just write me a cheque here and now. Let's do this!"

Now, we are talking about your money. What would you want to know? Again, the first thing that typically comes to mind is, "Are you going to really pay me back? And when?"

Why are you asking these questions? There's risk involved. Period.

Requesting finance involves risk. Let's get comfortable with the actual definition of risk. Risk is defined by Wikipedia as "the possibility of losing something of value. Values (such as physical health, social status, emotional well-being or financial wealth) can be gained or lost when taking risk resulting from a given action or inaction, foreseen or unforeseen (planned or not planned)."

Investors (friends, family, external investors) and lenders (financial institutions or groups) review business finance requests a little differently. However, the definition above covers everything.

When it comes to requesting finance, for any business, at any stage of growth, risk is inherent. The key to getting financing is first being aware of your risks and then, secondly, doing something about them, removing the risks completely or building a strategy to mitigate the risks

At any stage of the business there are six key risks to be aware of that directly relate to getting financing. They are as follows:

1. Character

Character and integrity of the applicant can be both subjective and objective.

- *Subjective:* review the reputational risk of this person, business, industry, type of product.
- *Objective:* review personal and business credit history, ensure that the business is operating within compliance and regulatory requirements, and has a strong strategic plan.

2. Collateral

What security will the company be able to put up should they not be able to pay the loan back? Buildings, equipment, accounts receivable, inventory?

3. Conditions

- Business: what is the purpose of the finance request? Is it for paying wages of the owners? Is it for new equipment that will increase efficiencies of the business, reduce costs and improve margins? Is it for working capital to help wait on receivables?
- Industry and economy: trending of industry and the economy.
- Operational risk: includes internal process risk (missing steps in a process) as well as external risk (environmental disaster).

4. Capacity

- What is the cash flow of the business? Cash flow is what will pay back the loan.

- Financial risk cash flow, too much debt, business focused on just one client vs. diversifying, or focused in one area vs. diversifying.

5. Capital

- Equity already injected into the business. Equity inside the business shows that you already believe in the business yourself by injecting money and/or building profits year over year.
- The ability to further inject into the business. Your ability to add more money into the business at a later stage (personal funds, personal loans, friends or family or investors).

6. Performance risk

For start-up businesses, there are more risks as you haven't yet "proved" that the business can be viable. In this stage, one key risk is performance risk. This is simply the probability that your service or product offering will work.

For example, if you are building a widget to enhance engine capacity, then how can you prove that your widget will perform? Likewise, if you are running a service business, how do you prove that your service will get the results you say it will?

Final thoughts

We have outlined some of the key risks involved in getting financing. In your business plans, you must clearly ensure that you have done the following: identify, assess, mitigate and monitor (ongoing) your risks.

If you want to build a business, you need to first understand the type of business you are building and why. Every business needs a strong foundation to stand on and grow. Once the foundation is established, you can then move to scalability and strategic growth.

Without a solid foundation, as you grow, you will see cracks, issues and potential tearing of the foundation and, yes, some do even collapse. Spending the time to build the foundation is indeed key to mitigating risk, raising financing and running a successful, profitable business!

Tennis and marketing are similar in that having a strategy is only part of the job; implementing the strategy puts the nail on the head.

Trish Mandewo

SEVEN

Marketing Strategies for Success

The heart of every business lies in marketing. The adage, "If you build it, they will come" does not apply in today's business world. It doesn't matter how great your product or service is, the success of your business depends on marketing. It goes without saying that marketing has evolved, and business owners need to adapt accordingly.

I love sharing a success story from Zimbabwe's first millionaire Clive Masiiwa, the mogul founder and executive chairman of Econet. This story is a testament to not only knowing your market but adapting and evolving with the market. Clive owns a diversified global telecommunications group with operations in 15 countries. When Econet unveiled their money transfer system, they came up with a cheap yet effective method to advertise this new technology.

They came up with a simple marketing plan: pay individuals to board transit taxis that run the same route between cities 24 hours a day. The people hired hop on during peak times, answer a call in the crammed taxi with eight to 12 people, and proceed to talk about how they had just sent money to someone in another city via cell phone, and how the money was available instantly. This was news to many on the taxis and they would all ask how this was done. The reps would provide details, hop out and catch another taxi and repeat the process. The Econet money transfer spread like wildfire in a very short time. Today, the company is the leading money transfer provider in many African countries. Masiiwa became Zimbabwe's first billionaire.

I like sharing this example as it shows how critical it is to know your market, know your buyer and devise a marketing plan that is specific for the audience. Today's buyer is very informed, and their characteristics certainly influences how you market and sell.

For a deeper dive on marketing, I turned to none other than the amazing Angela Bains, a professor at the British Columbia Institute of Technology (BCIT).

MARKETING: THREE CRUCIAL ELEMENTS

By Angela Bains

There are three crucial ingredients when it comes to marketing; understanding your audience in-depth, the personal touch of networking and the art of telling stories. Because at the end of the day, it's all about people. And that is what marketing should focus on.

The first thing you need when planning or thinking about marketing is a marketing plan. It is the master plan of how you will market your business. Keep it simple and don't over-complicate it. Your plan can be in a traditional report form or, as I prefer, chart form, much like a mind-map or flow chart. This chart then gets pinned up on the wall as a visual reminder so I can see it every day. Don't fall into the trap as I have done in the past of creating your marketing plan and then not following through because it is hidden away in a report.

As a business owner, life just gets busy and the consequence of this is no one looks at the marketing plan after it is written, and all that good intention gets zero action. However, if you are the report kind of person and that works for you then do what's right for you. Perhaps consider a combination of the two. Compile a written report which can then be summarized and turned into a chart that can be put on full display on your office wall so you see it every day. This will help you to be disciplined and follow through.

One of the other major aspects that causes a marketing plan to fall through is lack of investment. On average, you should invest five to ten per cent or more of your revenue, or if you are just starting your business, your projected revenue should be used to calculate your marketing budget. You should view your marketing budget as an investment not a cost.

In a nutshell, your marketing plan will outline the actions you want to take to attract potential customers or clients. It is important to do market research on your target audiences, so you understand them and their needs and how your business aligns with these needs. It is essential you put the customers or clients at the centre of everything you plan to do. Do not skip this step.

I like to get a little more detailed when it comes to customers or clients and develop personas. Personas are a detailed lifestyle of your ideal customers or clients. They are your central focus. Start by giving your persona a name, then move on to gender, occupation, salary, marital status, children, hobbies, music, food, fitness, political leanings, charities, donations, volunteering, etc. Also, cover the things they care about, and their values, status, environment, technology, self-esteem, fairness, justice. This is an excellent process for putting yourself in their position, thoughts, feelings and their life. What social media platforms are they on? What challenges do they have? What magazines do they read? What do they do to relax?

Once you have developed a persona, you can then move onto creating a journey map. A journey map is a typical journey your client or customer has before, during and after he or she comes into contact with your product or service. What are they thinking? How do they feel? What are they doing when?

Journey maps are used to explore:

- business processes (internally)
- company brand experience (how you deliver your service to your client)
- how people experience a business, service, product, system or process

For example, if I had a product called Mega Activity Kit for Kids and my persona is Debra a 38-year-old, mother of three school-aged children, I would journey map a typical day in the life of Debra. My journey map would reveal that she gets up earlier than her children to get a few things done before the children wake up. On my journey map my persona checks her social media first thing in the morning. This early period for example, 6:00 am to 7:00 am is then an ideal time for my company to run ads on social media. Once her children are awake, she is going to be busy in the mornings getting her kids ready for school, so she has no time to see my social media ads. I can then plan for radio ads for my products as she has the radio on in the kitchen once the children get up. When driving her children to school she listens to the radio, I can continue to run my ads on this channel. After she drops her kids off, she is back in the car and has free time. The journey map gives me a clear guide as to when and where to advertise my product.

The journey map also includes the following factors: three key motivators, pain and gain.

Let's look at each of these factors individually. For my persona, the three key motivators would be the following; she wants her kids to have an educational advantage, she needs to find activities at home to keep them busy, and she also needs some time to herself. I would then focus my marketing on the fact that my product is in keeping with these three key motivators as they are in keeping with her needs and my product can deliver on what she wants.

The pain in my persona's case is how is she going to keep her kids busy. The gain for her is creating some free time for herself or give light supervision while her kids are having fun with my company's product, Mega Activity Kit for Kids.

You can see how this example demonstrates targeting my customer or client just at the right times when they are available to see or hear my message. By using the key motivators, you can see what is on their mind and what drives them. You also identify the PAIN and market the GAIN. Use the journey mapping to identify opportunities or recommendations for improvements.

Your marketing plan will focus your mind on all the aspects you need to cover so your plan can succeed, and you are able to deliver what you promise. But remember, you MUST put your client or customer at the centre. It's not about YOU. It's about THEM.

Your marketing plan will cover:

- **Knowing your product** – what does it deliver.

- **Identifying your target market** – demographics include (a) persona(s) and journey map.

- **Your business advantage** – what makes you different and how do help your persona(s)?

- **The competition** – you need to know what they are saying and doing.

- **How you distribute or deliver your service or product.** How will you get your product or service into the hands of your client or customers?

- **The objectives** – is it to build awareness or increase sales by 10 per cent by a certain period etc?

- **Your action plan** – what you will do and how you will do it?

The key to this is YOU MUST TAKE ACTION! For your action plan you will make decisions such as what, when, where and how — will you use social media, advertising, networking, coupons, open house events, or perhaps use blogs to position yourself as an expert or problem solver? One of the best examples I have found of a company using a blog format successfully for marketing is an appliance parts supplier who has videos on how to install the parts you can buy from them online. Their reviews are amazing, and people really appreciate learning how easy it is to do these simple repairs themselves. They are considered the experts; people trust them, and they have had phenomenal growth and continue to expand their customer base by word-of-mouth marketing.

Networking – is still one of the best marketing tactics to market yourself and your business. The power of networking is you get to know people, make new business acquaintances and grow your business network. The purpose is to build relationships, not just land a client. The people you meet at networking events can both refer you and support you. Get involved in your business community and help it to grow.

Tell a short story. You have no doubt heard of the 30-second elevator pitch. The ones I have heard sound too contrived. No matter how much you practice, they come over as a sales pitch. Change your approach by telling the other person something so they will want to know more about. There are a couple of approaches that work well. One is in the form of a question. For example, in reply to the question, "What do you?" Reply as a question. "Have you ever had to wait in line, and someone jumps in the line in front of you?" They reply, "Yes, it's very annoying". You reply, "Well we develop digital customer service systems that prevents that."

The other response is in the form of, *don't market what it is, market what it does.* In reply to the question, What do you? You could answer, "We prevent arguments, fights and lawsuits." This naturally makes people curious. Then you can go to say, "We develop digital customer service tracking system that keeps people streamlined during waiting times."

Tell your story. People love to hear other people's stories about how or why they started business. Every story is unique and with its own challenges and adversity. I find you can learn so much from hearing other people's challenges. Telling your story can also be a great way to get some free publicity for you and your business. Local newspapers and magazines are often looking for interesting stories so if you have one you may want to approach them with an introduction about yourself and your business.

DO'S AND DON'TS

Do's

- Review your marketing weekly or monthly — consider chart form and pin it on the wall.
- Focus on your persona and do a journey map — put your client at the centre of everything you do.
- Build relationships with customers.
- Measure your return on investment and check your online analytics.
- Consider carefully which marketing channels you will use:
    - » face-to-face
    - » direct mail
    - » advertising
    - » email marketing
    - » social media

- » blogs
- » video
- » networking
- » personal phone calls (not cold calling)
- » building relationships
- » cross-promotion
- » speaking engagements
- » referrals
- » open house
- » taste testing, or try before you buy
- » guerilla marketing (get creative and do something different)
- » business card draw

Don'ts

- Don't develop a marketing plan and not follow through.
- Don't only use one form of marketing; there are lots of different channels you can use for your business.
- Don't use every form of social media, only the ones that make sense for your clients.
- Don't target everyone.
- Don't try too many things at once. Try, test and modify based on results.
- Implementing your marketing action plan is important, but knowing your audience is crucial to your success.

- Develop your marketing plan, commit to the investment, develop your persona(s) and journey map, and most important of all, take action! Here's to your marketing success!

> Social media is relationship building just as much as building personal relationships.
>
> **Trish Mandewo**

Social Media Strategy for Success

Social media can be defined as an interactive platform whereby people create and share information and ideas virtually.

According to the January 2019 wearesocial.com and Hootsuite Global Digital Report, the world's internet users were at 4.388 billion, 3.484 billion active social media users and 5.112 billion unique mobile users.

They also reported the following social platforms monthly active accounts:

Facebook – 2,271 million

YouTube – 1,900 million

Whatsapp – 1,500 million

WeChat – 1,083 million

Instagram – 1,000 million

With these statistics, it will be a dire mistake for a business to choose not to be present on social media.

When it comes to social media, most entrepreneurs, myself included, are predisposed to counting the number of fish in a flowing river. Because we know the impact of social media, we excitedly jump on board and quickly sign up for every social media platform there is. In 2009, a friend and local mompreneur Tera Loos of Smart-Mom-mies convinced me to join social media to showcase my then business Vancouver Tumblebus. Her point was that the young parents who were my ideal clients were all over Facebook and Twitter and I had to be there. Shortly after creating the accounts, I reached out to Laura Melvin who was the marketing person for the Tricities Chamber of Commerce. We met in a café for a Facebook and Twitter 101. Laura taught me the ins and outs of Facebook and Twitter in one-and-half hours, when to post, when to tag and how to link the accounts.

Between Tera and Laura, I quickly learned all the ropes and I was on my way to achieving social media success. Tera did e-introductions, tagged me on Facebook, and mentioned my business on Twitter. Not only was she my unofficial social media mentor, she wanted to see my business do well. What a selfless act this was. Thank you, Tera; the world needs champions like you who give and expect nothing in return. I am happy to say that I have paid it forward more than a hundred-fold.

I watched many YouTube videos, attended workshops and training like Hootsuite's social media training. I was like a sponge, absorbing all I could. Within a year, I had become a social media champ. I knew everything, including how Facebook calculates algorithms, and how to increase my Klout score. From there, I added LinkedIn and Instagram.

Just like in traditional marketing, you have to know where your audience is. Many people believe that if they create social media accounts, followers will automatically come. They also make the mistake of treating audiences on all platforms the same way. I learned early on to isolate the platforms. Here are some examples on how I approached social media with my Tumblebus business:

- **Facebook** – On this platform, I targeted young parents looking to plan birthday parties and events.
- **Twitter** – I used this platform to interact with businesses and to hold contests.
- **Instagram** – Here, I targeted young parents by showcasing the beautiful photos from events and birthday parties.
- **LinkedIn** – My goal here was to build relationships with businesses. I, in turn, turned the relationships into sponsorships.

My clientele from my business consulting side is very different. My focus is on LinkedIn, Instagram and Twitter. Though I love Facebook, my clients are generally not on that platform.

In case you are wondering how to choose the best platform, here is my 101:

1. Determine your intentions? Are you seeking to:
    - » Increase brand awareness?
    - » Network?
    - » Provide a platform for customers to reach you?
    - » Stay ahead of the competition?
    - » Business development by targeting a specific audience.
    - » Share content?
2. Know what each platform is for:
    - » Facebook is used by many to store photographs. It is a versatile platform, which is a great for relationship building, lead generation, targeted marketing and content sharing. Facebook's video content is one of the best.

- » Instagram: Mainly a photo sharing app with very little wording.

- » LinkedIn is for professionals. This platform is best for establishing your company as the trusted leader in whatever field you are in. Content is king here. You do not want to be selling to people here. If you are looking for a job or hiring professionals, this is your platform.

- » Twitter is a business-to-business platform (B2B) and its great for sharing snippets of breaking news, contests and giveaways, sharing photographs and sharing inspirational quotes.

- » Pinterest is all about food, décor, fashion, travel, images and more images. Do you want to show people how to do something or learn how to? Then head to Pinterest.

- » Snapchat: Mobile messaging application for sharing photos, videos, text and drawings. They have now added snap cash, a platform for users to send money.

3. Identify your ideal client and which platform they are using. Create your customer avatar. Infusionsoft wrote a good blog piece on creating an avatar and how to define your customer avatar. I incorporated some of their points here:

- » **Demographic traits:** List out your avatar's demographic traits (e.g., age, sex, education level, income level, marital status, occupation, religion and average family size). This area is typically easy to define.

- » **Visualize them:** Find a photo that closely resembles what your avatar looks like visually.

- » **Psychographic traits:** These are a little more complicated and require a deeper understanding of your customer avatar. They're based on values, attitudes, interests and lifestyle. Examples include wanting a healthy lifestyle, valuing time with family, using Pinterest to do home DIY projects.

- » **Name your avatar:** Naming your avatar humanizes the profile. If you are targeting both men and women, you'll want to create a male and female name.

- » **Data Collection:** Design a one-page collection of information about your ideal client

- » **Speaking of story:** Write one about your customer avatar. Imagine you are your avatar and are journaling about the discovery of your product or service. What were they thinking before they bought your product? How were they feeling? Why were they feeling that way? What were they looking for? What were they hoping to solve or accomplish? How did they find you or hear about you? How did they feel once they purchased your product or service?

4. Decide on content. What are you going to be sharing with the audience? No matter what choice you make, remember that content is king. You want to keep your audience engaged. When I post anything, I take time to create the post and I read it through to make sure it is professional and conveys the message I want the audience to get. Some people choose not to write their own posts but simply share:

   - » expert articles
   - » photographs
   - » videos
   - » quotes
   - » funny content

- » testimonials
- » events / webinars

The most important thing is for you to choose how you want to show up and what you want to convey.

My favourite platform is LinkedIn. I have facilitated a few workshops on how to effectively use LinkedIn. I feel that that most people do not fully understand LinkedIn and they underutilize it.

As I shared above, LinkedIn is the best platform for B2B marketing and for establishing your company as the trusted leader in whatever field you are in. There are many benefits if this platform if used correctly. Here are a few:

- Organic lead generation that sprouts from the focused, relevant and unique content that you share.
- Elevate your profile by receiving skill endorsements and recommendations.
- Marketing Funnel Automation by drawing clients into your circle of influence.
- Ability to join professionals' groups and network with them.
- Opportunity to inspire your current and future clients by sharing stories and successes.
- Stay at the top of connections lists by utilizing the sponsored In-mail.
- Pivot your company as the credible and trusted source by sharing your expertise.
- Build your network by connecting on a professional level with others who will be of benefit to you either now or in the future.
- Use the LinkedIn groups as a resource and think tank for information and brainstorming.

- Access to jobseekers and recruiters.

LinkedIn Definitions and housekeeping items that you should know:

- **LinkedIn etiquette** – LinkedIn is all about reputation. There are a few things that are considered good practice such as having a professional headshot, personalizing connection and recommendation requests, responding to private messages promptly and nurturing relationships. As a rule, I do not accept any requests to connect from a profile that has no photograph.

- **Connections** – Connections are other registered users who you know personally on LinkedIn. Although you can invite anyone to be a connection, they will need to set up an account to use the site.

- **Second-degree connections** – These are the connections that your connections have. If you are connected to me and I, in turn, am directly connected to Lexi, Lexi will be a second-degree connection for you. Looking at other people's second-degree connections is a way to grow your own circle. You can always ask them to introduce you.

- **Third-degree connection** – Once you are connected to Lexi as a second degree, any connections that she has will be third-degree connections to you.

Once you are all set on LinkedIn, remember to build relationships. Comment on your connection's posts, make referrals, post expert articles, ask for recommendations, give recommendations. I watch a lot of people on LinkedIn who post and not a single person likes or comments. If you notice this, do a review to ensure you are posting relevant content. Avoid gossiping and negative attacks. Speak to the issues at hand. If in doubt, do a test post and see if you get responses or traffic from it. Most of all, know your Klout Score. Klout is a website and mobile app that uses social media analytics to rate its users according to online social influence.

Go forth and enjoy your social media platforms.

Knowing my brand was like an upward drift that helped me soar even higher

Trish Mandewo

Know Your Personal Brand

We all have a personal brand, an identity by which we market ourselves. If you are curious to know what your brand is, just ask your inner circle and acquaintances what they say when you are not there. Making a conscious choice to finetune your brand will tell the story in your own words; after all, people buy people and their stories, not products. It is critical to build a personal brand that takes into consideration your purpose, your passion and your personality.

A few years ago, Diana Bishop helped me define my brand as an "Opportunity Crusader." Being able to articulate my brand helped me gain confidence in who I am as a businesswoman.

According to Carnegie Institute of Technology, "85% of your financial success is due to your personality and ability to communicate, negotiate, and lead. Shockingly, only 15% is due to technical knowledge." If you will retain anything from this chapter then make sure it's the fact that you are unique, talented, passionate and that your story is the road to your success!

Here are my top "P" rules on personal branding:

- Give yourself **P**ermission to be you.
- Allow your **P**ositive qualities to shine.

- **P**osition yourself for growth and differentiate yourself from your competitors.

- **P**ivot – Be known for something. What is your story?

- Define your **P**urpose. What makes you tick?

No one understands personal branding better than the "Story lady" aka Diana Bishop. Here is what Diana had to say.

DEVELOPING YOUR PERSONAL BRAND
By Diana Bishop

Companies invest a lot of time and effort on developing their brands. Why shouldn't that be true about people? Just like your company's brand is built on defining and packaging what makes it special and unique, I believe personal branding is also about packaging ourselves to reflect who we are and what we stand for at our very core.

In fact, think of your personal brand as *your competitive edge* to help differentiate yourself in a crowded marketplace. Consider real estate, financial services, coaching, consulting, interior design, selling clothing, hardware or software. With so many people in each of these areas selling similar things, consumers are overwhelmed with their choices. If they can put a face to the business, know where the passion comes from and understand that you have specialized knowledge or expertise that they need or want, they look at that as an important selling feature.

Entrepreneurial icons know this. When Steve Jobs came back to Apple in the mid-'90s, he decided it wasn't enough to make products, he needed to sell *his* excitement for creating devices that would actually change the world. Others like Oprah Winfrey, Ralph Lauren, Sheryl Sandberg, Bill Gates, Mark Zuckerberg and yes, even Kim Kardashian, are also all hugely successful because each one of them not only creates products and services, but they have built definable values and passions into those things.

Now, we can't all be in their league, but having your personal brand is not about being famous. Everyone has a personal brand. The key is to *define* and then *leverage* your personal brand to attract the audience with whom you want to do business.

Many people confuse personal branding with hiring an image consultant, creating a new website and starting a Facebook page. That is what I call physical branding. It is important but it comes later. Personal branding is conceptual. It starts with understanding what is the one thing that you are really good at. I mean really, really, really good at! Let me give you a couple of examples.

I will start with myself. I was always telling stories as a kid. I think that is why I became a journalist. I was a TV news correspondent for 20 years travelling the world telling a new story every single day and I loved it. But then suddenly, after 20 years, I decided I wanted to do something different and start my own communications business. I had always been especially passionate about the successful people I met and interviewed, from presidents and prime ministers to movie stars, Olympic athletes and even ordinary people doing extraordinary things. So, I decided that what I was really good at was helping people tell their stories to become even more successful. I like to name things so I called myself a "Success Storyteller." That, as it turned out, was how I now describe my personal brand. No surprise that I eventually called my business The Success Story Program™ and people identify me as the "Story Lady." It really helps differentiate me. That's personal branding!

Consider also my friend Dan, the lawyer. Dan worked at a big law firm where he confessed to me that he didn't really stand out because there were floors and floors of other lawyers more or less just like him. I asked Dan, "So what is the one thing that you are really good at?" He told me he loved the world of business and particularly helping business owners set themselves up legally for success. In fact, he said he seemed to be one of the only lawyers driving new business like that into the firm. However, he added he was not getting any recognition for this.

I said to Dan "It sounds like you are a "'Deal Catalyst.' You act as a catalyst to bring in new deals to the law firm." "That's right! That is exactly what I am, a deal catalyst," beamed Dan. Dan then took this new information and approached the firm's partners with a plan. He offered to take the lead on new business development. The partners were thrilled because it meant more money in their pockets. Dan continued to do what he has always done, but because he had packaged himself around his unique ability, he got to do more of it and his reputation began to soar, raising his profile and growing his reputation. That's personal branding.

This can work just as well if you are an accountant, a dentist, or selling running shoes or cars. Let's say you are in the home furniture business and your passion is creating custom crafted furniture. So perhaps you are a "Woodworker Crusader" on a crusade to help people preserve the ancient art of woodworking. You can build your personal brand (and your business) by promoting your expertise in this area, perhaps by holding workshops, blogging, and creating online videos with tips, tricks and secrets for fellow woodworking enthusiasts. That's personal branding.

We are all selling something. And we all have knowledge and expertise related to or around what we are selling. That is what we need to package if we are going to be successful in this brave new world. Here are four tips to help you get started toward developing and promoting your personal brand!

1. **Identify your personal brand.** Synthesize what you are really, really, really good at. Give it a name. This makes it tangible. Re-

member that it must speak to your expertise. Here's another important factor; it is always, always, about *how you help people*. Personal branding is not about you! It is about how you can be of service to help others.

2. **Re-work your bio.** Every business owner or entrepreneur needs a bio that they can use on a website or other social media platforms, and/or to send out to prospects. So, tailor your bio to include what you have learned about your personal brand in #1 and thread the concept through your accomplishments.

3. **Update your LinkedIn page.** LinkedIn is a key tool for any businessperson. It is where most people will go to find you, so make it stand out. Put the information from your new bio from #2 in the Summary section near the top of the profile. You might want to also revamp the descriptions of your various work positions as well.

4. **Develop your elevator speech.** Every business owner needs a clear, concise and *interesting* infomercial to let people know what you do and why they should care about it. Imagine the difference between someone who starts with "I am a communications specialist" or "I am a Success Storyteller." Which person would you want to get to know? It always works for me.

So, get out your branding iron, tell your story and watch your success soar to new heights!

"When the path gets darker and hope fades, a mentor is there to remind you to keep your eyes open and look ahead as the darkness is only temporary.

Trish Mandewo

TEN

Mentoring for Success

Mentoring can simply be defined as a professional relationship in which an experienced person willingly guides someone less experienced. This relationship helps the less experienced person develop specific skills and knowledge that will enhance their professional and personal growth.

I have gained so much from mentorship (formal and informal). When I had my businesses in the United States, I had no mentors. I turned to family and friends, most of whom didn't have much to offer as they had not walked the walk. I had to go at it alone. Luckily, as a resourceful person, I read and researched a lot and I survived. In Canada, my journey has been totally different. I have been lucky to have mentors such as Mike McCarthy, vice president of Telus Business Solutions for Western Canada; Laura Patrick, owner of Kids Physio; Jack Unger, regional sales manager for RBC Royal Bank; Elder Matias of Mighty Oaks Business IT; and Reece Sims of Reece Sims Branding & Strategy, to name a few.

Sometimes you meet people who become informal mentors and you learn so much from them even if you are not really scheduling mentoring sessions. I had a few of those: Carolyn Cross, owner of Ondine Biomedical; Barbara Mowat and the rest of the Vancouver Grow your Biz board; Cecilia Mkondiwa of Women's Enterprise Centre; my amazing husband, my late dad, my mom and many more.

Jack Welsh of General Electric is credited as one of the pioneers for **reverse mentoring,** which refers to an initiative in which older executives are paired with and mentored by younger employees on topics such as technology, social media and current trends. Jack did this in 1999 and had great success.

There are many reasons why everyone needs a mentor regardless of age. Here are some reasons why. Mentorship:

- Provides insights about the nuts and bolts of running a business or personal journey.

- Pushes you in the right direction and helps you define your goals.

- Provides emotional support and keeps you focused.

- Provides a sounding board and someone to actively listen.

- Gives you constructive feedback and possible solutions or actions from someone else's perspective.

- Helps you avoid making the same mistakes — why not get it right the first time?

- Provides a source of inspiration and hope.

- Helps you save time. Having a mentor forces you to be more organized.

- Keeps you accountable; we all achieve peak performance with accountability.

- Avails you of a personal consultant and advisor all in one.

I got one of my mentors through Vancouver based Forum of Women Entrepreneurs (FEW). I reached out to the founder Christina Anthony for some insight on mentoring.

THE POSITIVE IMPACT OF MENTORSHIP

By Christina Anthony

Running a business can be hard, lonely, and challenging. It is not always an easy journey but having a mentor can help you keep your focus, gain some perspective, provide clarity and offer much-needed support. In fact, access to a mentor can be the difference between a stagnant business, and one that is connected, strategic and growing.

At FWE, we strongly believe in mentorship and on its positive impact on entrepreneurs. At the heart of our mission stands a tradition of valuable engagement by industry experts and experienced business professionals. These leaders instill accountability and increase motivation among mentees to continue overcoming challenges and reaching your goals. Whether you are starting a new venture, experiencing unexpected growth or questioning your exit strategy, benefits of mentorship are undisputable. As we heard from many entrepreneurs over the years, mentors can be wonderful sources of knowledge, compassion and guidance. For example, they can encourage you to be more confident in your decision-making, as well as taking the steps needed for your business to move forward. They can offer insightful feedback and relentless encouragement to help you advance in the right direction. Most of all, they can be there when you need someone to talk to.

Receiving one-on-one guidance can be a game-changer as it also provides accountability and reflection on accomplishments and challenges. At FWE, we emphasize working *on* your business rather than *in* your business. You probably have heard this countless time, but have you ever truly taken the time to look at the bigger picture? As an entrepreneur, there are so many things to do in the day-to-day operations and it can be hard to catch your breath. This is when your mentor comes in. They can ask the right questions to help you decide which path to follow, which steps to take or which door to open. True mentoring is non-directive. Successful mentors teach their mentees the problem-solving process rather than giving them the answer to a particular problem. As experienced leaders, they freely donate their time to provide feedback and ideas. They are a precious source of information and can be the key to a successful business. It's up to you to make the most out of a mentorship experience. As we like to say, you will get out of it what you put into it.

Mentorship is not only valuable from the receiving end; it's also incredibly rewarding for mentors. They sometimes learn alongside mentees, which can even ignite some new ideas for their own professional journey. As one of our mentors once said: "I want to start all over again! Old dog, new tricks." Get inspired and pay it forward. We call that a win-win! You also get to make a real business impact, while becoming a valued part of an entrepreneur's career and journey. Plus, who doesn't want good karma? Mentorship is also a great way to not only extend your network, but also create meaningful relationships. These can be crucial to your business' success. So, what are you waiting for? Succeed. We dare you!

Christina Anthony collaborated on this piece with Melodie Gingras and Larkin MacKenzie.

MORE ON MENTORSHIP

By Women's Enterprise Centre

Women's Enterprise Centre (WEC) is another organization that provides mentorship. The CEO Laurel Douglas and Executive in Residence Cecilia Mkondiwa are good friends and advisors to me and they have played a big role in my journey.

Mentors can provide not only practical insights about the nuts and bolts of running a business, but emotional support as well. A business mentor knows from experience what knowledge might be missing and how it feels during the first years to believe in the business and keep moving forward despite the challenges. Kaityln McConnell, mentoring manager at Women's Enterprise Center knows the benefits of mentoring and she sees it first hand. WEC has summarised all things mentorship well. Here is an insert from their website.[5]

Mentors benefit from:

- Feeling pride as they share vicariously in their mentee's growth and development.

- Increasing their own knowledge as they take on a task that may require them to exercise new skills.

- Experiencing increased professional recognition for volunteering their time.

- Experiencing professional renewal as they guide their mentee through challenges.

- Expanding their own networks.

- Feeling satisfaction in helping others to avoid mistakes they may have made themselves.

- Acting as a role model to other women in business

Role of the mentor:

- Takes a long-range view on your growth and development.

- Helps you see the destination but does not give you the detailed map to get there.

- Offers encouragement and cheerleading, but not "how to" advice.

- Provides non-judgmental support.

---

5 www.womensenterprise.ca/business-advising-mentoring/mentoring/

- Provides guidance on issues raised.
- Speaks from your own experience rather than give advice.
- Helps clarify goals of mentee.
- Passes on their knowledge and experience.

What does a mentor do?

The following are among the mentor's functions:

- Teaches the mentee about a specific issue.
- Coaches the mentee on a particular skill.
- Facilitates the mentee's growth by sharing resources and networks.
- Challenges the mentee to move beyond his or her comfort zone.
- Creates a safe learning environment for taking risks.
- Focuses on the mentee's total development.

> If your employees are disengaged, it's a direct reflection of your leadership or lack thereof.
>
> **Trish Mandewo**

Show others that you care by stepping into their world and getting to know what makes their heart smile

Trish Mandewo

ELEVEN

Human Capital

A few years ago, I participated in the E-series program which was offered by Forum of Women Entrepreneurs (FWE). There were over 80 women business owners at this three-day intensive training. I remember vividly that in our group, the second most prevalent problem everyone was facing after financial capital was human capital. For small to medium businesses, the human capital problem is magnified as most cannot afford to hire a human resources manager.

Everyone dreams of hiring the perfect team so that they can work on their business and not in the business. I know this because I am one of those. I have had three service businesses, a home health agency, a janitorial company and a kid's mobile gym. All my businesses were staff-dependent and very time-sensitive. Looking back, I have no idea how I managed to not have high blood pressure over the years.

Anyone who asks me about the challenges of being a business owner is met by the answer human resources. For 19 years, I lived on the edge, wondering daily if I was going to receive a call from a patient or their family complaining that the nurse or home health aide did not show up, a call from an angry office manager telling me that their office was not cleaned or buffed, or that a three year old was standing by the window waiting for the Tumblebus to drive up and it never did. All these scenarios happened at least once. As a result, my husband and I always had our shoes ready so we could run to the job site at any given moment. As a business owner, you have to do your best to ensure that the client is taken care of.

I will also take the opportunity to apologize for bending the truth in some instances when my back was against the wall and I didn't know what to tell the client. Often, the problems came when I hired in a hurry, when I didn't have the choice to wait for the ideal candidate. The worst hire was when I hired someone who was using clients phone to make international calls. How do you catch that behavior in an interview?

There were many joys as well. I knew that staff were the face of all my businesses, so I treated them well. I made sure I trained them well and I did all I could to retain the good ones.

For many companies, employees come and leave as fast as they came in. The state of disengagement is at an all-time high. But how can you retain your good employees? How can you keep them engaged? I turned to my good friend Jennifer McKinnon, owner of Creating Culture, on building the "want to" in employees. Here is what Jen had to say.

HUMAN RESOURCES

By Jennifer McKinnon

The dictionary defines human resources as "managing resources related to employees," or "overseeing the various aspects of employment and business operations in compliance with employee and employer's standards and expectations." Maybe you will find that it specifies the duties pertaining to the position such as benefits, recruitment, performance evaluation, etc. If you ask me, I'd say HR builds the "want to" in employees; employees wanting to go to work, wanting to be better, to be more educated, wanting to be the best for their company. When we help create these employees, we create culture. And culture is key.

What is not commonly mentioned in organizations is the benefit of businesses providing employees with someone to talk to; an open door to trusted confidentiality. HR can provide a gateway to a personal experience that offers advice to inspire culture, engagement and motivation for an employee in their place of work. I cannot stress enough the significance of employers seeing employees as their most critical business asset. Workplace culture can be just as crucial as your overall business strategy as it can make or break your organization.

Last year, Forbes wrote an article on the way HR can help create a sustainable company culture. "Solid company culture is key for any business. It determines how engaged your employees are and for how long you are able to retain them. As a human resource professional, your responsibility is to help shape your company culture so that it is sustainable over the long term." We as HR need to find those individuals who align with our company's values and then find ways to motivate, engage and empower them to be their absolute best.

If you do some research, there are some pretty amazing statistics out there when it comes to employee culture and engagement, and I challenge you to do so. As reported by Talent Culture, engaged employees reported an average of 2.69 sick days annually per employee, whereas companies with weak engagement efforts report an average of 6.19 according to the Workplace Research Foundation. And here's another one for you: Dale Carnegie reported that companies with engaged employees, outperform those without by 202 per cent! Needless to say, the concept of culture and engagement in companies will become not only useful, but vital to the success and profitability of your organization.

The relevance of HR in business today is more imperative than ever. Organizations thrive on customer service and competitive advantage. A time where human capital is everything and retention is key. For small business specifically, where employees are cross trained to carry out multiple responsibilities and are accountable for a variety of aspects of different departments, the impact of losing one individual could be detrimental to the organizational effectiveness, culture and bottom line. Having the right individual to take care of your hiring, training, coaching and developing of your people can help you build great contributors to your business.

There are many HR functions that are critical to a business, but being available, having that structure of communication and implementing solid workplace practices with employees is so valuable. Create that effective leadership, enhance your performance management, give feedback and recognition; really construct that durable employee engagement and culture. Those essential pieces that HR can provide small business will directly impact attaining and retaining that human capital necessary for sustaining and growing businesses and their bottom line.

TWELVE

Taking Care of Your Biggest Asset

As discussed in the previous chapter, hiring the right people is critical. It is true that employees are your biggest asset. Many managers and business owners know this, and they probably tell their employees how they value them once a year at the annual party. But … is that enough? When I was an employee many years ago, my response was always, if you appreciate us, show us how; what are you doing or what have done to show your appreciation? I know I wasn't the only one with these questions.

Richard Branson said it best when he stated that clients do not come first, employees do. From the first day I had an employee many years ago in Oklahoma, I made sure they felt valued and welcome. I remember times when my employees did not speak English and I did not speak their language, but I did everything I could to get to understand them on a personal level. It was not uncommon for me to walk around with dictionaries in other languages. I was willing to do anything to ensure that they felt that they were part of the company. My goal was always to get them from using phrases like "your company" to "our company." In many cases I was very successful.

My biggest wins were when their families felt as though they were part of the company even though they were not my employees. I always made sure I involved the family members in all celebrations.

It was not uncommon for me to call a bowling party or a barbecue at the lake to celebrate staff. I knew what my employees liked. For all my companies, my full-time employees stayed with the company until I sold it. This is a big testament to how they felt about the company. In the case of the Tumblebus, my longest standing employee ended up buying the business.

One other practice I believe in is having regular employee-led meetings. The employees make the agenda, but two items are always a MUST: what's working and what's not working. In these meetings, I got to really know my staff and what makes their blood flow or boil. Sometimes, the meetings were tense at the beginning, but everyone always left smiling at the end. Everyone felt heard and understood.

Many small to medium businesses make the mistake of not celebrating their employees as they feel that they are too small to do so. You don't have to be a big company to appreciate your employees; it starts with that one employee that you have. Create the right culture and the rest will follow.

For all the years that I was running my last two businesses, my sister Kanu Jacobsen implemented Providence Health's largest key initiative for the State of Oregon. She created a comprehensive and sustainable employee engagement strategy. She worked with senior leaders to develop strategies and demonstrable links between engagement and strategic goals. She ran workshops focusing on "appreciation in the workplace" for medical home teams including physicians, managers and frontline staff. She also developed, designed and implemented a physician resilience program to reduce physician burnout. Who better for me to turn to for an expert piece on appreciating your biggest asset than my little sister!

UNDERSTANDING YOUR EMPLOYEES

By Kanu Jacobsen

In my previous job, I traveled across Oregon and Washington doing employee engagement and working with the C-suite and high-level managers. I had many tools in my toolbox but specifically, I noticed the transformations that were happening when the languages of appreciation were used well. I had firsthand experience. It goes without saying that I highly recommend the languages of appreciation. It solves a lot of pain points in the workplace. Using Languages of appreciation can prevent small problems from potentially blowing out of proportion. Here is an example from one of the teams I worked with.

> *A senior manager had very high expectations on her staff. The staff shared with me that she was very demanding. Staff also mentioned that they would go above and beyond to meet her needs, but she would not appreciate them at all. The phrase "THANK YOU" would never come from her mouth. Every time the team met, the manager would bring baked goods that she personally made without taking into account anyone's dietary constraints. This was causing a lot of conflict and tension on the team. The manager was very confused as to why her staff felt unappreciated. After working with the team and identifying everyone's languages of appreciation, it became clear that they were not communicating with each other appropriately. They learned a lot about each other, and the outcome was positive for all.*

Why is it crucial to appreciate employees in the workplace? Well, as a business owner you will battle with recruiting and keeping the best and brightest. One of the biggest expenses a company will incur is employee turnover. Gallup has done many studies over the years and it is estimated that up to 80 per cent of employees who quit site lack of appreciation as a key reason for leaving their jobs. It is highly crucial that you make an effort to show recognition to your employees before they leave for your competitor.

When employees do not feel appreciated, they exhibit some negative cues: discouragement, irritability, resistance and unexcused absences. They make the environment negative for everyone else and productivity goes down. Individuals in the workplace need to feel appreciated in order to enjoy their job, do their best work, have positive work relationships and stay with their organization long term.

In another Gallup study, only one in three workers in the US strongly agreed that they received recognition or praise. This goes to show you that the problem is more prevalent than we think. Do you know how to appreciate your employees?

No one understands the power of *The 5 Languages of Appreciation in the Workplace* more than Dr White, the co-author of the book. I have had the pleasure of working closely with Dr White and I have learned a lot. When implemented well, the five languages method helps management to effectively communicate, appreciate and encourage their employees. The result is higher levels of job satisfaction, healthier relationships between managers and employees, and decreased cases of burnout.

There are five languages of appreciation that can help you understand your employees: words of affirmation, quality time, acts of service, gifts and physical touch. Physical touch, however, can be tricky with the workplace's rise in harassment cases. Bringing the Languages of appreciation workshop into your company is simple. Each employee will take the assessment, at the end, they will know their primary, secondary and least valued language. This will help rid of blind spots and improve team dynamics.

Here is a synopsis of the five languages.

1. Quality time

This language is where we give undivided attention to our coworkers or our employees. This entails focused attention, companionship, shared experiences, personal connection through listening and sharing. The amount of time desired can differ significantly depending on whether it is with colleagues or with a supervisor.

2. Acts of service

This is a language of collaboration as it involves physical assistance in the form of receiving and giving. Some examples include helping your employees or getting them help to get ahead, working collaboratively on a project that would be difficult to do alone, or just working alongside with them on a task.

3. Tangible gifts

This language can be tricky but if done right it can be appreciated. The key is the effort and thought behind it not the amount spent. Taking time to notice what your employees enjoy. Do they like chocolate? coffee? music? or movies? I personally like to show others my appreciation by bringing unique souvenirs from my travels around the world. My colleagues quite enjoy the gifts. It doesn't have to be a store-bought gift; it can be something you made.

4. Words of affirmation

All communication is not created equal. This language is particularly important as it has many moving parts. Of importance is how the message is conveyed, the tone used and the timing. Words of affirmation can be both oral, written, one on one or in a group setting. It is critical to know the preference of the subject you are dealing with. Creating a culture of recognition and affirmation will foster a fun, bully free and positive environment.

5. Physical touch

Employees that appreciate this language often use high fives, fist bumps and professional handshakes to express their sentiments. Other forms such as hugs might be deemed inappropriate. It is important for boundaries to be set and for employees to know what is appropriate and what is not.

Appreciating your employees is crucial to your business bottom line. Businesses that have invested time and money into creating a culture of appreciation get to enjoy a positive work environment, dedicated and engaged team members resulting effective performance.

As Stephen Covey said next to the physical survival, the greatest need of a human being is psychological survival. People want to be understood, affirmed, validated and appreciated. The 5 languages will cover the psychological need and will make your job much easier. Go forth and appreciate your greatest assets.

THIRTEEN

Emotional Intelligence for Business Success

There are many types of leadership out there. Growing up in Zimbabwe, we didn't have names for the leadership styles. I look back now and notice that both my Mom and my Dad had very high intelligence quotient (IQ) and emotional intelligence (EI). They successfully passed these qualities to their seven girls. For that, I am so thankful. My husband and I are doing our best to raise our daughter with both said qualities. In 2018, I took the EQ-i 2.0 assessment with the guidance of my then business partner Sandra J. Horton. Here is a synopsis of the report on Happiness, Independence and Leadership.

Happiness: Trish, your result in Happiness suggests that you almost always maintain a happy disposition towards all aspects of your life. You enjoy the company of others and are likely on a positive life course where your happiness is seen and experienced as infectious. Your results in Happiness and the four most connected subscales are high. Because of this, you likely experience a certain balance between your well-being and optimism, self-confidence, personal relationships, and fulfillment of goals. Gains in one area likely contribute to gains in another — quite a reciprocal set of relationships! You may exude cheerfulness at both work and play while participating in activities you truly enjoy. Be seen by your team as motivating and resilient in the face of obstacles.

Independence: Trish, being independent means, you are capable of feeling, thinking, and working on your own, a critical skill that all great leaders have in common. Your results show that this is a well-developed skill, as you are willing and capable of holding your own ideas and making necessary decisions required for your team on your own. You are unlikely to be swayed by popular opinion, which can help you maintain an established direction for your team. Consider the following interpretation of your results: You are comfortable providing direction and working on your own. You can work without emotional dependency on others, and don't require their reassurance. You accept responsibility for your decisions, knowing that at times people will disagree with you. Be cautious that you don't appear so independent that your team feels you overlook their feedback and involvement. You scored well above average on Independence and fall within the leadership bar.

Leadership: Your leadership approach embraces change and values innovation from your team. You are likely seen trying new methods in both your leadership skills and the processes you use to get work done. Your leadership is steadfast and decisive even in high pressure situations. Your team looks to you for leadership and guidance, although you may need to be mindful that some people may not cope as well with pressure as you do. Your result on this subscale is not only above average but also falls above the leadership bar.

No one I know is more passionate about emotional intelligence than my friend Sandra J. Horton. I am thrilled to have Sandy's contribution on why it is important for leaders and business owners to be emotionally intelligent.

THE IMPORTANCE OF EMOTIONAL INTELLIGENCE

By Sandra Horton

Leaders are 70 per cent more likely to succeed in business when they lead through an emotionally intelligent lens. Emotional intelligence (EI) is the single best predictor of performance in everyday workplace and is one if not the strongest drivers of leadership and personal performance. Leaders who understand and embrace the four domains of EI (self-awareness, self-management, social awareness and relationship management) will build strong, secure and trusting relationships in their personal lives and business world. EI leaders make better decisions, communicate successfully with others and manage stress more effectively. Sounds great, right? The EI Toolbox provided below will give you eight practical practices to build your emotional intelligence for superior business accomplishments.

Think about an outstanding leader, mentor or friend. Some examples of outstanding leaders are Michelle and Barack Obama, Oprah Winfrey and Warren Buffet. When you think of these individuals, what descriptive words come to mind? What makes them outstanding? The true secret is their high emotional intelligence.

Some descriptive words that come to mind are that they are all self-aware, strong relationship builders, good listeners, caring, empathetic, inspiring and visionary thinkers. All these traits are some of the personal abilities or skills that form one's emotional intelligence. Many consider these the "soft skills" of leadership and are, in fact, attributes of EI leaders. The great news is that you too are hard wired to have emotional intelligence and you can grow in your EI throughout your entire life. Your success in business depends upon it.

Emotional Intelligence Toolbox for Success

The EI Toolbox's practices work together to support emotional intelligence competency development and personal leadership growth. These eight practices can be implemented one at a time or in combination. You probably already do many of these practices or perhaps not. These eight practices work together and there is no wrong way to approach them. They are:

1. Be open to self-exploration

Getting to Know YOU! You are your own best expert. You are the only one who discerns what it is like to walk in your shoes. Here are a few suggestions to start your journey of self-reflection. You can tackle one or more of these strategies as you see fit.

Start by identifying your personal core values these are ideals that you want to live your life by. You pursue examples such as openness, trust, courage, independence and integrity. Next, clearly define how you will show these core values to your employees, friends and family daily. For example, "I will actively listen to my employees' concerns by reframing their concerns and help them find a solution alongside them." This shows that you value openness.

The next task is to reflect on your personal interactions with people for one week. It is best if you select both a personal and professional relationship to explore. Use a journal to capture your interactions. Try to identify and record your conversation focusing on words said and reactions felt. Pay attention to any unusual feelings or peculiar conversation stoppers. Try to define three personal areas that stood out for you from those exchanges.

Once you have these recorded transactions, select one of those interactions that stood out for you and ask a friend or colleague, "What one piece of advice could you offer me to improve (in this particular area) that would help me in the future?" This practice is very impactful and will yield a lot of personal information for your reflection.

Oddly enough, by investigating your outward interactions, you will begin to absorb more about your own inner self. These actions will build your self-awareness, which is one of the critical domains in emotional intelligence.

2. Manage from the heart

Leadership anchored from a heart-centered approach is one from within yourself. First and foremost, you must learn how to check in with yourself and to listen to what you are feeling. You, as a leader, must learn to ask yourself, "Does the feeling I have now and the subsequent actions I am about to take, align with what I know is right and true?" Your answer to this question is critical and should be answered with a firm, "YES"!

A heart-centered approach is powerful and certainly not weak! Your ability to simply feel and open up to yourself is unquestionably powerful and not faint. Listen to how your emotions and your self-talk show up and how you naturally express yourself. Be alert to your "heart signals." These inner-centered signals emerge in important decision-making times that may seem, well, not quite right. Heart signals transpire in situations and trigger in the past or present, at the same time giving you insight into your body or emotional triggers. Learning your heart signals will make you overall more self-aware. Mindfulness allows you to be able to hear yourself and is essential to leadership and personal growth.

The abundant news is that by starting and living from a heart-centered place will raise your emotional intelligence in areas of self-perception and emotional self-awareness. Self-awareness is defined as, "The ability to be sensitive to one's own emotions, and understand their impact on us," which was made famous by the work of Daniel Goleman, *Emotional Intelligence: Why it can matter more than IQ, 1996*. Managing from the heart allows you to manage and share your feelings in a way that supports constructive positive self-expression.

3. Power of perspective

Perspective is powerful. It guides you and enables you, but it can also limit you. In any given point in time, perspective can be viewed as a particular attitude or way of thinking. It frames how you respond to situations both personally and professionally. Perspective is informed and directed by our past understanding plus perceptions of those experiences.

In business, as in life, by consciously being more aware of your moments you are in you can STOP! Then reflect! You can ardently be in the present, in the here and now, which will transform your life. Focus on what is in front of you by selecting to be more mindful and aware. Be observant of your thoughts first, along with the emotions attached to the circumstances. Emotionally intelligent leaders understand the power of perspective and learn to manage their responses. They learn to balance and direct their levels of emotional reactions like assertiveness, empathy, emotional self-awareness and impulse control. Perspective impacts all four domains of EI equally.

Consider a real-life example of your last crucial conversation with a business colleague or employee. How did you perceive the individual, the situation or the outcomes? Were they as you wanted or hoped to achieve? Ask yourself why you are thinking a particular way? What story are you telling yourself?

4. Acknowledge your quiet leader

Sitting quietly and patiently, a highly successful EI leader watches their team's interactions. Only when they have had time to understand her own feelings and their own emotions at play does the patient leader wait for the ideal time to speak of the situation dynamics and the needs of the team.

Emotionally intelligent leaders know that this is *the* tactic they need to succeed. For some leaders, this may not be so easy. The consequences of not being a patient, quiet leader when situations warrant can be disastrous. Consider the perspective from the lens of an individual team member. When confronted with a leader who speaks all the time without listening, they can see that leader as being weak or a bully. Disengagement will take place because they feel unheard and unvalued. On the other hand, if a leader practices patient, quiet leadership, and evokes their observer and listens to understand self, others and the situation, the leader will be seen as being supportive, strong, a better problem-solver and someone who cares for and values their people.

To help you answer the leadership question, "What can I learn or observe of myself in this moment?", and as efficacious starting practice to evoke your quiet leadership, this routine can be used:

- First acknowledge your own need to speak.
- Stop, breathe, find a way to catch yourself.
- Reflect and ask yourself these three questions:

1. Why am I needing to speak now?
2. What emotions are driving me to action?
3. What is the outcome of my actions on others?

Doing so you will improve your relationships, your leadership and your own emotional intelligence. Use these principles repetitively to set a new course forward and to reverse any flawed actions, which might benefit both you and the other persons. One pronounced gift you give yourself is to acknowledge that you don't need to always speak or be heard.

5. Lead the way forward

Leaders lead the way forward. You take a stand for what you think is right even in situations where you may be the only one who does! You find solutions to problems even when others may not. However, you may do both alone and in collaboration with others. Through engaged conversations of what matters most to others, you lead with true empathy and concern.

In EI leadership, you inspire others to follow your vision, which then becomes a shared vision for your organization. With mindfulness, you "walk the talk" and support change. These are all foremost behaviours that emotionally intelligent leaders convey when they are leading the forward way. Actively engaged with others you lean in to be understood and encouraging. EI leaders are true to their word and seek ways to balance personal needs with the needs of others. Naturally, leading can be challenging and perplexing. Facing the unknown requires personal self-regard, self-actualization and courage, attributes of emotionally intelligent leaders.

Dare yourself to build these skills perhaps just one at a time. To not do so, you risk the probable consequences of being seen as a frail leader. It is your choice to make and which paths to follow as you lead yourself forward.

6. Live with a sense of gratitude

As a business owner or leader, living with a sense of thankfulness is a crucial and critical outlook to have. Gratitude causes the growth in your feeling of thankfulness and appreciation in your personal and professional world. Gratitude is unlimited for the giver as well as the receiver. Becoming a high performing EI leader means that you have the capacity to do both. Gratitude toward others can take many forms and be delivered in many ways.

Honest thankfulness and acknowledging others is powerful in leadership of small or big teams. Being open to input from others and valuing them through gratitude is indeed incalculable.

7. Learn daily

Life teaches you lessons and to learn from them is vital. Emotional intelligence is truly all about learning. Emotional intelligence is earnestly gaining knowledge about yourself. It is openness to new information. To challenge yourself to grow daily as leaders and individuals is certainly a contest. Only you, the owner of your individual perspective of any given situation, can check in to see if your current reality is true.

You can learn something that either reinforces your own thinking and feeling or explore new ways of being. Be vulnerable to learning from others and yourself. Trust others and be authentic by showing them the same presence and respect. EI leaders can learn so much from the little things if you have the right perspective to see it. Emotionally intelligent leaders, who take a learning position coupled with a heart-centered approach, will find boundless attainments in business.

8. Give back

To build the practice to give back, you need to consider your own intentions to give. It is a powerful practice that yields considerable change in your life if practiced humbly and not just dutifully. A leader's life is busy and demanding by daily giving in the work.

The practice is one of giving back to others. The intention is to give outside of self and direct it to others. There is a disparity in truly giving of self and the giving of your time that is task or focused outcome. Ask yourself, "What can you give of yourself that helps others grow?" Giving to others will support your personal growth in so many ways and levels. Your levels of self-actualization and interpersonal relationships will evolve positively impacting overall personal growth.

Being able to build relationships is key to success personally and professionally. Relationships require a commitment to give and take. A leader understands these keys and seeks to understand other people's perspective. All leaders, regardless of where they fall within the organizational chart, learn that this is best achieved by becoming aware of themselves, their emotions and how they drive their behaviour and actions. Smart and emotionally intelligent leaders learn to control themselves and wait to respond until they have the chance to clear the emotions out of the way.

Overall, leadership growth can occur slowly or quickly. The key is to stop, reflect and seek a new perspective. These eight practical practices if actioned out, will build leadership capacity to becoming an emotionally intelligent leader. At its core, emotional intelligence specifies suitable ways to: enhance and understand one's innate self and how they function, recognize the reasons behind why you are controlled by emotions, and offer new insights into yourself plus live a more balanced and self-aware life. In applying these eight tips outlined in this emotional intelligence toolbox, you too will be on your way to becoming an effective emotionally intelligent leader and business owner.

Putting your heart and soul into business is not a choice, it's a necessity.

Trish Mandewo

Being organized quiets the mind and sharpens the brain for peak performance.

Trish Mandewo

FOURTEEN

Trish's Toolbox

My father, Cyril Mupfuuri Masenda, was one of the most well-read people I have ever known. He believed that knowledge was power, but more so, he believed that hoarded knowledge was of no use to anyone. He believed in sharing everything he knew. Needless to say, I am quite my father's daughter. I love researching and I am always open to learning from others. Like my father I believe that *power is not in the knowledge we have but in sharing with others.*

As a serial entrepreneur, I have had my fair share of entrepreneurial experience. Like my father, I truly believe in sharing knowledge. This is why I was inspired to write this book. This chapter is a compilation of some of the things I often share. It hurts me when I see business owners, especially start-ups, making the same errors. So far, we have covered the main topics, and here are a few more tips that are critical but are normally ignored.

1. Have a strategy

Business strategy is the art and science that enables organizations to achieve their goals and objectives. Business strategy gives you the direction and a road map for success. When starting a business, you need a launch strategy. If you are an existing business, you need a growth strategy. Entrepreneurs need to think and plan strategically so that they can stay one step ahead of their competition. An organization that lacks a strategy and a sense of purpose risks being pulled in many directions. It's like stepping on the tennis court without a plan: you are bound to lose. I certainly was there before.

The key to success for Small to medium enterprises (SME) in today's market is to have strategic and ensure it's actioned out. As an "Opportunity Crusader," I can speak to this. A lot of SMEs mistakenly take financial budgets and projections as strategy. A strategic plan covers four of the most important questions: What, Why, When and How. Start off by setting your vision and mission if you don't already have one. If you have one, re-visit it as things are constantly morphing in business.

Move on to setting SMART Goals. Your goals should describe your intended impact.

S = Specific: Having specific rather than overarching goals will help increase the chances of you attaining the goals.

M = Measurable. We all know that if you measure it, it will happen. You need to identify exactly what the outcome will be. see it! hear it! feel it! Defining the manifestations of your goal or objectives helps you visualize them. The best way is to evaluate your success at reaching targets is to use KPIs. A **key performance indicator (KPI)** is a measurable value that demonstrates how effectively a company is achieving key business objectives.

A = Attainable: Don't set yourself up for failure. Spend ample time reviewing whether your goals are within your means as far as financial and human capital.

R = Realistic. Shooting for the stars is okay but why do you want to reach this goal? What is the objective behind the goal? What will your business look like after you achieve it?

T = Timely. Plan everything, use your time effectively.

If going through strategic planning on your own is daunting, there are many companies you can hire. These goals you set are your roadmap and they will help you succeed. Think through them and be realistic. Here is a S.M.A.R.T. goals template to get you started.

GOAL	STATE YOUR GOAL.
Specify	How are you going to achieve this goal? Who needs to be included? When do you want to do this? Why is this a goal important?
Measure	How will you measure your progress? How will you know that the goal has been accomplished?
Achieve	How can the goal be accomplished? Do you have the skills required to achieve the goal? What are the logical steps to take to accomplish the goals?
Relevant	Why am I setting this goal now? Is it worthwhile? Is it aligned with the overall vision and objectives? Do I have the necessary resources?
Timely	How long will it take? What's the deadline? Is it realistic?
S.M.A.R.T. Goal	Review what you have written and craft a new goal statement based on what the answers to the questions above have revealed.

2. Treat your business plan as a living document

Most business owners often talk about their business plan being a living document, but for many, its nothing but! Most business owners do the business plan for purposes of funding, or at the beginning, and then forget about it.

Business metamorphosis starts from the day the door opens and the targets shifts constantly. Competitors come in, marketing tools change, policies and procedures change, industry legal and risk factors change. The key to success is to continuously innovate and make your product or service better than yesterday so you can always be one step ahead of the game.

All these factors are an indication that the business plan needs to be fluid, much like a tennis match; one walks on the court with a solid plan. One factor that is an unknown is the game play from the other side. Being fluid allows the player to make slight adjustments while staying with their game plan. Business is not much different.

If I am to be honest, I would have been one of those business owners who never look at the business plan if I didn't have a business adviser. She made me look at the numbers and at my business plan constantly. If you are someone who needs someone to hold you accountable, I highly suggest getting a business advisor.

3. Be a master time manager

William Penn said it best, "Time is what we want most but what we use worst." Most of us realize and affirm that time is an asset, and yet we have no plans and no direction when it comes to spending it? I used to be one of those entrepreneurs who worked 16 hours a day. I was the one who when asked how I was, my answer would be "very busy." Rightly so. I had no life. In my second year of Vancouver Tumblebus, I remember working long and hard hours to the point of exhaustion. The tipping point was when one day I decided to go for a walk along the river. I got my headphones and made sure my favourite playlist was on my phone. About 15 minutes into the walk, I was getting very irritable, the music was actually making noise. My brain was on overdrive and the music was interfering with my thoughts. The problem was that I was living and breathing my business and I could not turn my brain off even if my life depended on it. I clearly could not identify whether I was coming or going. *I had lost control of time and I was losing my mind in the process.*

I knew I had to do something about this. In my research on how other entrepreneurs were handling time management, I discovered the Pareto Principle and the 80/20 rule. Italian economist Vilfredo Pareto first wrote about the Pareto Principle in 1895. He noticed that people in his society seemed to divide naturally into what he called the "vital few," the top 20 per cent in terms of money and influence, and the "trivial many," the bottom 80 per cent. In time management, this rule can be interpreted to mean that 20 per cent of the work you do should produce 80 per cent of the result. You should therefore focus on the 20 per cent of the items that will have the biggest impact and shelf the small stuff, better yet, delegate the small stuff.

I decided to try this method. This meant that I had to spend time on my TO DO list. I did a weekly list and a daily list. I had to go a step further and prioritize the tasks. Which 20 per cent of work was critical? What result was I expecting that week? What was my goal?

My favourite app is Accomplish. I get to add all my tasks and I cross off or delete completed ones. Any pending tasks automatically get moved to the general list. From the general list, I can drag any tasks to a specific day and time. I add tasks in the moment. I used to add them at the end of day and found out I was missing some especially after long days. I have a friend who absolutely loves Rabbit Task App. I tried it and it wasn't for me. There are many other free ones out there. Choose the right one for you.

Here are my top tips on time management:

- Plan your work focusing on the top three most important tasks you want to accomplish.

- Avoid procrastination.
- Learn to say NO.
- Delegate whenever possible. This includes personal, family or business-related tasks.
- If tasks are too big, break them down into achievable chunks.
- Be in control of your time.
- Take a balanced approach.
- Multitask only when necessary. Multitasking can add stress and deter you from completing tasks.

Debriefing Template

P-RULES	QUESTION	RESPONSE
Progress	What worked	
Problems	What didn't work	
Plan	What should I change?	
Pivot	What can I reinforce?	
Prepare	What are the objectives for the following week?	

The bottom line is that if you don't plan your year, month, week or day, someone else will plan it for you. Jim Kwik says creating routines in the morning and evening helps him insulate himself from decision fatigue. Which means you can only create a finite number of good decisions each day. Setting up habits early in the day creates positive momentum and a vision and direction for your day. Besides a to-do list, Jim Kwik also creates a to-feel list. He makes three professional goals and three personal goals for the day. He goes on to say that he decides how he wants to feel as he doesn't want to feel a certain way by accident but rather by design. That's powerful. I personally don't make a "to-feel" list but I set positive intentions in the morning and that sets my emotions for the day.

Making a to-do or to-feel list is good and dandy, but a lot of people don't use the list effectively. Here is a list of don'ts that can help you focus:

- Do not procrastinate.
- Refer to the list often after making it.
- Remember to put personal goals on the list.
- Work smarter, not harder
- Put only what you can accomplish in 24 hours.
- Use the 20/80 rule and focus on the most important tasks.
- Take breaks; your brain needs a break to be efficient.
- Close email and texts alerts, they can be huge distractors.
- Celebrate every success along the way.

5. Pick the right price point

It is safe for me to assume that we all agree that product or service pricing is one of the most important business decisions a business owner must make. It is so critical because clients want the best deal, and the business wants to make a profit.

When I launched Tumblebus, I had no pricing model to go by. I knew what they were charging across the U.S. and in Toronto. Vancouver being a different market, I had to make sure I chose the right pricing point. I am not embarrassed to say, I still got it wrong even after I did all my homework. I ended up making two price adjustments in the first year. I learnt quickly that if you start too low, it will be very difficult to raise the price as clients will get used to paying a lower amount. I was however scared that I would not get any business, so I chose a "safe" price.

In many cases, customers shy away from telling businesses how great the service or product is as that might mean the business will raise the price. In my case, clients could not stop talking about how great the Tumblebus was and how great our staff was. The feedback did indeed give me confidence to raise the prices and to create more packages.

The goal in pricing is always to have a good markup to cover overhead expenses and generate enough profit. The trick is that there are always other overhead expenses that we miss at the beginning. Pricing for products is less daunting than pricing for a service. For a service, the expenses are more subjective whereas for goods it's pretty much selling goods for more than what you paid.

For my Tumblebus business, I didn't have the original price nor direct competitors to reference. I also didn't have an idea of how much diesel, bus maintenance and repairs cost. After the first four to six months, it was clear that I had to adjust my prices thereby changing my bottom line.

Here are my top pricing tips:

- Know all your operating expenses, both direct and indirect. Understanding the true cost will help you determine the hourly rate if you are a service company. For products, the true cost added to your purchase price will provide the base charge. Don't forget to include your salary in the expenses!

- Decide what net profit margin you want. The general rule of thumb is that anything between 10 per cent and 30 per cent is healthy depending of course on what industry you are in.
- Do your research. You need to be aware of direct and indirect competitors' prices.
- Know why your price is what it is and communicate it clearly to your clients.
- Don't undersell the value of your product or service. Your clients will need to understand the value of your service and expertise. If you don't help them understand, they will default to their perceived value.
- Remember that pricing is more of a psychological game than a numbers game.
- Know your numbers. Monitor profitability on a monthly basis. If it's not your forte, then get someone else to help you.
- When your clients start commenting about what a bargain for the value, it's time to adjust your pricing.
- Be discreet and strategic. Raise your prices after winning an award or after launching something new. If you drive a lot, raise your prices after a gas price increase etc. Customers are less likely to complain if you take a strategic approach.
- Never discount to make sales, only add value. Don't compromise on price.
- If you are a service, stay away from discount sites such as Groupon.

Avoid these pitfalls

- Not putting an email signature at the bottom of your email.

- Being complacent and not anticipating changes in the marketplace.

- Not knowing your online reputation. Whether your business is active on social media or not, your clients are, and they are talking about you. Especially talking about your shortcomings. You should focus not only on managing and improving your reputation but also work hard to maintain a good image.

- Not having your company name, phone number and email address on Facebook and LinkedIn.

- Not knowing your financials. Knowing your numbers is critical for your business success.

- Not celebrating your successes.

- Overpromising and underdelivering.

- Selling yourself short. Don't be scared to tell a client why they should choose your company.

- Do not depend on emails and calls solely. A face-to-face meeting is still the best.

- Don't swim in murky waters. Lack of clarity is a detriment for small to medium businesses.

- Selling the product instead of selling an experience.

- Not Surrounding yourself with people who are better than you.

- Done is better than perfect. You can read and plan all you want. The act of doing is the most important one.

> Success lies in setting your goals and relentlessly pursuing them! I dare you to succeed.
>
> **Trish Mandewo**

EPILOGUE

The inspiration behind writing his book was solely to share with you a wealth of information and business experiences that you can immediately implement in your quest to grow your enterprise and satisfy the hunger for success. Do not stop shooting for your goals! There is no one formula to run a business but there are common pitfalls that we face. You now have them all in one place together with ways to minimize and manage them. Adapt these to your needs and goals and you are on your way to running an efficient, growth-oriented organization that will survive the ever-changing business environments you find yourself in. Embark on your journey and remember not to travel alone.

AUTHOR'S BIOGRAPHY

Trish is an accomplished entrepreneur, Speaker, Facilitator, City Councillor for City Coquitlam, and principal of Ubuntu StratEdge, a company whose purpose is advancement of women on boards as well as culture and diversity in the workplace. She is a driven, innovative and passionate leader. Trish also Co-founded Women's Collaborative Hub Society, a personal growth and empowerment platform where women acknowledge, own and share their gifts.

Trish is an award-winning entrepreneur. On the personal side, she is most proud of being named 2017 RBC Top 25 Canadian Immigrant and being awarded the Canada 150 Sesquicentennial pin for leadership and community service.

Trish graduated from Oklahoma Baptist University and The University of Central Oklahoma in the fields of Medical Microbiology and Embryology. Trish considers herself a savvy serial entrepreneur as she has successfully built 4 businesses as well as a nonprofit. She believes in sharing all the knowledge she has gained in the 20+ years she has been an entrepreneur.

Some of her accomplishments includes being Panelist and advisor for Telus Small Businesses and best practices for engaging Today's savvy customers, being featured on Chek TV Reality TV show - "The Hardway Show". She has been highlighted in several other media outlets. She is a sought-after speaker locally and internationally and she loves incorporating her own life and business experiences in her speeches and workshops.

To book Trish as a speaker,
or facilitator, visit:

www.trishmandewo.com

Connect with Trish on:

Facebook: www.facebook.com/TrishMandewo

Instagram: www.instagram.com/trishmandewo/

Twitter: twitter.com/TrishMandewo

LinkedIn: www.linkedin.com/in/trish-mandewo-1929a560/